WCARTs CO

Recipes and Fine Art by the Artists of the Warren County ARTs organization
Warren County, New Jersey

www.WCARTS.ORG

Cookbook Compilation: Pamela Eden

Cookbook Contributors (recipes and/ or artwork):
Pamela Eden, Ruth Grabner, Kathleen Jusko, Shirley Spangler
Marie Gelsomino, Maureen Heritage, Jody Cooke, Peggy Niece
Carol Southerland, Kathy Rupff, Deette Little, Pat Olds
Merle Morse, Patti Tivnan, Jean Marie Perry, Gordon Perry
William Reynolds, Susan Reynolds, Carol Zielinski, Caroline
Goldsmith and Annie Robertson

WARREN COUNTY ARTS

The Warren County ARTS (WCARTS) started in 1992. Our mission- as an organization is to promote the advancement of the arts in Warren County, New Jersey and provide venues for artists with a variety of programs. Our goal is to provide the community with an opportunity to experience many artistic disciplines. Warren County ARTS welcomes anyone who is an artist, wants to be an artist or just enjoys hanging out with artists. Our meetings are at 7pm the second Thursday of every month (except July or August) at the Oxford Municipal Building in Oxford, NJ. Each meeting has an exciting program to stimulate and educate. We offer two members-only shows a year along with many opportunities to participate in a solo or group exhibit in the Oxford Municipal Gallery.

Warren County ARTS is a not for profit 501(c) (3) organization. A membership form is included at the back. Membership includes a monthly newsletter mailed (or emailed) directly to you, a personal gallery page on the WCARTS.org website and free entry in various member-only shows each year. Single membership is $25 per year and $45 per year for a family membership.

Gordon Perry

~ History of the Warren County ARTs organization ~

Warren County ARTs (WCARTs) is a group of artists located in Warren County, New Jersey. The Warren County Cultural & Heritage Commission and George Warne spurred us to start an artist's group in 1992. Our first meeting as a group of artists was at Shippen Manor in Oxford when we selected our name and elected officers. Jeffrey Kuhlman was the first President. We met for a while at the President's house, but in order to grow we needed a more public space. Member Peggy Niece was on the Board of the Warren County Technical School at the time and secured approval for the group to hold the monthly meetings at the school. We became a legal nonprofit organization not long after that. Our first member show was held in the Oxford Municipal Building in September 1996 and represented all 16 members. It was called Artistic Visions. Those first members were Duane Alpaugh, Jill Bateman, Stan Cohen, John Delonas, Elaine Erny, Al Hough, Jeffrey Kuhlman, Deette Little, Merle Morse, Peggy Niece, Mary Schwartzkopf, Grace Scodari, Carol Southerland, Jack Stephens and Albert Young. Happily many of these early members are still participating in the group today.

The show was such a hit Mayor Don Niece asked if we could do it on a regular basis to which we agreed. We asked Mayor Niece if we could use the Municipal Building for our monthly meetings because we thought that it would be nice to meet where our art was hanging. We have continued since that time to have two Member shows and two Open Shows plus a number of individual exhibits every year. Our first Open Show (open to non-member artists) was called Think Spring and it was held in the Spring of 1997.

We now have over 30 members and hold monthly programs with guest or member artists giving demonstrations or lectures in a variety of artistic media (music, dance, poetry, fine arts and fine handcrafts). A monthly newsletter is published providing information about the current and upcoming exhibitions, programs, member news and artistic opportunities available outside the group. Those interested in joining the WCARTs group are encouraged to complete a membership application-available from our website: www.WCARTS.ORG. Funding for our programs is made possible, in part, by a grant from Warren County Cultural & Heritage Commission.

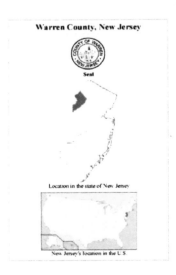

Warren County, New Jersey

Seal

Location in the state of New Jersey

New Jersey's location in the U.S.

Pamela Eden

Table of Contents

Chapter 1: Breakfast

Kathy Rupff

Blueberry Muffins

Cook Time: 20 minutes
Recipe from Jody Cooke

Yield: 12 muffins

Switch out regular flour with rice flour for a wheat free treat.

1-1/2 cup flour	**1 egg beaten**
1/2 cup sugar	**1/2 cup milk**
1 tablespoon baking powder	**1/4 cup melted shortening cooled**
1/2 teaspoon salt	**1 pint blueberries**

Into a mixing bowl, sift flour, sugar, baking powder, and salt. In a separate bowl, whisk together egg and mil. Stir egg milk mixture into the dry ingredients. Stir in cooled melted shortening, stirring just until ingredients are blended. Fold in blueberries. Spoon batter into 12 generously greased muffin cups filling 2/3 full. Bake at 400F for 20 -25 minutes.

Makes 12 medium sized muffins.

Cornbread Tamale Pie

Makes 6 servings

Cook Time: 45 minutes
Recipe by Pamela Eden

I use a skillet that has a lid and can go from the stove top into the oven - so I just have one pot to clean.

1 pound ground beef	**CORNBREAD**
1 onion chopped	**3/4 cup yellow cornmeal**
1 (8-ounce) can cream of tomato soup	**1 tablespoon flour**
1 cup water or stock	**1 tablespoon sugar**
1/4 teaspoon pepper	**1 1/2 teaspoons double-acting baking powder**
1 teaspoon salt	**1/2 teaspoon salt**
1 tablespoon chili powder	**1 beaten egg**
1 (8-ounce) can whole kernel corn drained	**1/3 cup milk**
1/2 cup chopped green pepper seeds &	**1 tablespoon vegetable oil**
membranes removed	

Pre-heat oven to 425F

Saute the ground beef and onion in a large lightly greased skillet until meat is highly browned and the onion is translucent. Add soup, water, spices, corn and green pepper. Simmer 15 minutes.

In a small bowl, sift and mix the dry ingredients for the cornbread. Moisten with the egg and milk. Mix lightly and stir in the vegetable oil. Transfer the meat mixture to a greased 2 quart casserole and cover with the corn bread mixture. The topping will disappear into the meat mixture, but will rise during baking and form a layer of corn bread on top. Bake about 20 -25 minutes or until corn bread is brown.

Easy Cheese Danish

Preparation: 10 min, Cook Time: 20 min

Yield: 8 Danish

Recipe from Pamela Eden | Source: foodnetwork.com

8 ounces cream cheese, at room temperature
1/3 cup sugar
2 extra-large eggs yolks, at room temperature
2 tablespoons ricotta cheese
1 teaspoon pure vanilla extract

1/4 teaspoon kosher salt
1 tablespoon grated lemon zest (2 lemons)
2 sheets (1 box) frozen puff pastry, defrosted
1 egg beaten with 1 tablespoon water, for egg wash

Preheat the oven to 400 degrees F. Line a sheet pan with parchment paper. Place the cream cheese and sugar in the bowl of an electric mixer fitted with a paddle attachment and cream them together on low speed until smooth. With the mixer still on low, add the egg yolks, ricotta, vanilla, salt, and lemon zest and mix until just combined. Don't whip! Unfold 1 sheet of puff pastry onto a lightly floured board and roll it slightly with a floured rolling pin until it's a 10 by 10-inch square. Cut the sheet into quarters with a sharp knife. Place a heaping tablespoon of cheese filling into the middle of each of the 4 squares. Brush the border of each pastry with egg wash and fold 2 opposite corners to the center, brushing and overlapping the corners of each pastry so they firmly stick together. Brush the top of the pastries with egg wash. Place the pastries on the prepared sheet pan. Repeat with the second sheet of puff pastry and refrigerate the filled Danish for 15 minutes. Bake the pastries for about 20 minutes, rotating the pan once during baking, until puffed and brown. Serve warm.

Frittata

This can be made in an frying pan capable of going into a 425F oven.

1 large zucchini cut into bite size pieces
1/2 purple onion
butter

10 eggs
crumbled goat cheese

Melt butter. Chop 1/2 onion and add to hot butter. Add salt & pepper. Add zucchini and brown to remove moisture. Crack eggs into bowl. whisk with salt & pepper. Add eggs to pan with zucchini and cook until outer edge sets. Add crumbled goat cheese on top. Put pan in 425F oven til completely set on top.

Kathy Rupff

Granola

1/2 cup firmly packed brown sugar
1/4 cup unsulfured molasses
1/4 cup honey
1/4 cup water
3 tablespoons vegetable oils
2 teaspoons cinnamon
3 cups old fashioned oatmeal
1/2 cup raisins

1/2 cup coarsely chopped walnuts
1/2 cup coarsely chopped pecan
1/2 cup coarsely chopped almonds
1/3 cup flaked unsweetened coconut
1/3 cup sunflower seed
1/4 cup wheat germ
2 tablespoons sesame seeds

Combine brown sugar, molasses, honey, water,oil and cinnamon in heavy small saucepan. Bring to boil over low heat, stirring constantly.

Preheat oven to 325F. Combine oatmeal and all remaining ingredients except raisins in large roasting pan. Drizzle syrup over, stirring to coat mixture thoroughly. Bake until toasted stirring every 10 minutes, about 40 minutes. Add raisins before storing granola. Cool granola completely store in airtight container in cool dry place. Serve with lowfat milk or yogurt or just eat straight out of the jar!

Overnight Cherry Almond Oatmeal

Preparation: 5 minutes, Cook Time: overnight
Recipe by Pamela Eden

4 cups vanilla almond milk
1 cup steel cut oats
1 cup dried sweet cherries or mixed dried
  berries

1/3 cup packed brown sugar
1/2 teaspoon salt
1/2 teaspoon ground cinnamon

Note- this recipe is great because I can make it in the slow cooker on Sunday night and have enough oatmeal for breakfast throughout the week.

Mix ingredients together in 3 quart slow cooker coated with nonstick cooking spray.
Cover and cook on low for 7 -8 hours. Serve warm with regular milk or almond milk.

Patti Tivnan

Soy Scramble

Preparation: 5 minutes, Cook Time: 6 minutes

Recipe by Pamela Eden.

This recipe calls for exactly 1 carton of tofu, so there's no last bit left in the carton to be thrown away or languish in the refrigerator.   Thanks to a pinch of turmeric, tofu can masquerade as eggs in any scramble. Try it with toast at breakfast, wrap it in a tortilla for lunch or serve it with rice for dinner.

14 ounces firm tofu
2 teaspoons extra virgin olive oil
1/2 medium red onion
1 large red bell pepper stemmed, seeded & thinly sliced
6 ounces cherry tomatoes halved

1 1/2 teaspoons fresh thyme chopped
1/2 teaspoon ground turmeric
3/4 teaspoon coarse salt
1/2 teaspoon freshly ground pepper
1 ounce freshly grated Parmesan cheese
2 tablespoons fresh chives chopped

Place tofu on a rimmed baking sheet lined with paper towels, then cover it with a layer of paper towels. Place a baking sheet on top, and press to remove as much liquid as possible.. Crumble tofu into 1 inch pieces. Heat oil in a nonstick skillet over medium high heat. Add onion and bell pepper and cook until softened about 3 minutes. Stir in tofu, tomatoes, thyme, turmeric, salt and pepper, and cook for 3 minutes. Stir in Parmesan and 1 tablespoon chives. Sprinkle with remaining chives and serve immediately.

Spicy tomato eggs

Recipe by Pamela Eden

I had this one morning at a B&B in Italy. I bumped up the kick with the Delmonte "zesty" diced tomatoes that have jalapeno peppers, but you could just as easily use any can of diced tomatoes. Include some nice juicy sausages and toast and this is a breakfast that will satisfy.

1 (14 1/2-ounce) can zesty diced tomatoes   **4 large eggs**

Heat a tablespoon of oil in a skillet and add the can of diced tomatoes. Heat to boiling. Crack eggs and gently add eggs to the tomatoes happily bubbling away in the skillet. Allow eggs to poach to desired doneness before serving eggs and tomatoes with sausage and toast.

Chapter 2: Starters

Cheesy Zucchini & Red Onion Flatbread

Cook Time: 25 minutes
Recipe by Kathleen Jusko

1 (10-ounce) package refrigerated pizza dough
3/4 cup garlic & herb cheese spread divided
3/4 cup finely grated Parmesan cheese divided

3 tablespoons fresh Italian parsley chopped
1 small red onion
1 zucchini cut into 1/8 inch pieces
olive oil

Pre-heat oven to 400F
Line a baking sheet with parchment paper, spray with nonstick spray. Spread 1/2 herb cheese over 1 long half of the pizza dough leaving a 1/2 plain border, Sprinkle with 1/2 of Parmesan and 2 TB parsley. Using Parchment as aid, fold plain half of dough over filled half. Spread remaining herb cheese over top. Sprinkle with remaining Parmesan. Remove outer layer of onion to yield 2 inch core. Cut into 1/8 inch rounds. Arrange 1 row of zucchini down 1 side of dough. Arrange onion round in row alongside zucchini. Arrange 1 more row zucchini alongside onion. Brush vegetables with olive oil, sprinkle with salt and peper. Bake until puffed and deep brown at edges, about 25 minutes.

Clams Casino

Recipe by Kathleen Jusko

6 ounces clams with liquid
1 cup bread crumbs seasoned
4 tablespoons olive oil

French bread thinly sliced
garlic powder to taste

Blend all ingredients in a pie plate. Put under broiler until bubbly. Serve on thin sliced French bread.

Italian Caponata

Cook Time: 24 hours
Recipe by Kathleen Jusko

1 small eggplant peeled & diced
1/2 cup onion chopped
2 tablespoons olive oil
2 medium tomatoes chopped
1/2 cup red and/or yellow pepper chopped
3 tablespoons red wine vinegar

2 tablespoons tomato paste
1 teaspoon sugar
1/2 teaspoon salt & dash red pepper
1/2 cup sliced black olives
1 tablespoon dried parsley (or basil)
1 tablespoon drained capers

In a large skillet cook eggplant and onion in hot oil til tender. Stir in tomatoes, sweet peppers, wine vinegar, tomato paste, salt & pepper. Cook uncovered over low heat 3 minutes. Stir in olives, herbs and capers. Cover and chill 24 hours. Let stand at room temp for 30 min before serving.

Maryland Imperial Crab

Cook Time: 30 minutes
Recipe from the Kitchen of Shirley Spangler.

Yield: 1 dozen

Crab artwork also by Shirley Spangler

1 pound fresh or canned crab meat (lump)
1 egg
8 squares saltine crackers crushed finely
3 teaspoons heaping mustard yellow

3 tablespoons heaping miracle whip
mayonaise
dash salt and pepper
1/2 teaspoon dried parsley flakes
dash Worcestershire sauce

Mix all ingredients together reserving some cracker crumbs for tops. Put mixture in either glass crab shells or custard cups equally. Sprinkle with remaining crumbs and parsley flakes. Dot with butter. Put into a pan with some water and bake at 350F for 30 minutes or until lightly brown.

Note: can add sprinkle or two of Old Bay Seasoning or use on the side for extra flavor.

Mini Caprese Bites

Recipe from Patti Tivnan

grape tomato
mozzarella cheese balls

fresh basil sliced lengthwise

Skewer one of each ingredient on a toothpick
Drizzle 2 Tablespoons each balsamic vinegar and olive oil, sea salt and freshly ground black pepper over each mini skewer.

The Falls
in
Blairstown,
NJ

Gordon Perry

Gordon Perry

Roasted Pepper Mozzarella Rolls

Cook Time: 20 minutes
Recipe by Kathleen Jusko

red bell pepper   **mozzarella cheese**
Pre-heat over to 350F.

Slice peppers apart along their creases. Remove seeds and roast peppers on parchment line cookie pan till charred. Remove from oven and cover wth waxed paper and a dish towel until cool enough to handle. Peel skin from each pepper. Into each piece of pepper, place a 1 inch square of mozzarella cheese and roll up in pepper.
Place pepper-cheese roll-ups close together in baking dish.   Bake 20 minutes until cheese melts.

Three-in-one Cheese Ball

Recipe from Marie Gelsomino

Cream Cheese Ball   **1/3 cheese mixture**
1 (8-ounce) package cream cheese softened **1/2 cup crumbled blue cheese**
4 cups shredded Cheddar cheese   **fresh parsley minced**
2 tablespoons milk   **Garlic Cheese Ball**
2 tablespoons onions chopped   **1/3 cheese mixture**
dash black pepper   **1/4 teaspoon garlic powder**
Blue Cheese Ball   **paprika**

In a mixing bowl beat the softened cream cheese, shredded cheese, milk and onion until the mixture is fluffy. Divide mixture into thirds (~ 1 cup each).
Shape 1st portion into a ball, roll in pepper. Add the blue cheese to the 2nd portion, roll in parsley. Add garlic powder to the third portion, roll in paprika.

Cover and refrigerate cheese balls. let stand at room temperature before serving. Serve with crackers.

Uncle Kenny's Kicker Cheese Spread

Recipe from Carol Zielinski

2 pounds velveeta Cheese   **1 pound bacon cooked**
1 jar horseradish sauce   **3-5 drops hot pepper sauce**
1 cup mayonnaise

Melt cheese according to box directions. Cook bacon and break up into bits.
Mix Cheese, mayo, bacon and hot sauce together and spoon into ceramic bowl. CrockPot or decorative serving dish. Cover and refrigerate until cold.

Serve with your favorite crackers.

Chapter 3: Salads

Patti Tivnan

Bean Salad

Recipe by Deette Little

1 (16-ounce) can kidney beans	1/2 cup white wine vinegar
1 (16-ounce) can cut yellow wax beans	1/2 cup olive oil
1 (16-ounce) can garbanzo beans	1/2 teaspoon dried mustard
1 (16-ounce) can cut green beans	1/2 teaspoon dried tarragon
1 green bell pepper thinly sliced	1/2 teaspoon dried basil
1 onion thinly sliced & separated into rings	2 teaspoons dried parsley
DRESSING	1/2 teaspoon salt

Drain and rise the cans of beans. Layer in a large bowl and top with the green pepper and onion slices. Mix dressing ingredients together and pour over the bean mixture.
Cover and refrigerate. Stir occasionally to coat all beans with dressing mix and before serving.

Blue Cheese Dressing

Recipe by Kathleen Jusko

2 cups mayonnaise	1 teaspoon celery salt
1/4 pound blue cheese	2 cloves minced garlic
1 teaspoon sugar	1 can evaporated milk

Mix all ingredients together with electric mixer until cheese is at the desired lump size.

Cabbage Salad

Yield: 2 servings

Recipe from Pamela Eden

When Thanksgiving and Christmas dinner comes around - I remember how much I would look forward to having this salad -because it was the only time when my mother would make it. I've lifted that restriction and make it much more often. Its a great side for a dinner or a just a sandwich.

1/4 cabbage thinly sliced & chopped	1 - 2 tablespoon onion finely diced
2-4 large dollops of mayonnaise	

This is a nice fresh & crunchy salad. It does not store well, so don't make too much at once.

Thinly slice and chop the cabbage into a glass bowl. Add finely diced onion. Add enough Mayonnaise to coat the cabbage. Add a dash of salt & pepper and mix well.

Crab with Crisp Bitter Greens

Recipe from William Reynolds

1 head Belgian endive
1 head chicory
3 cups arugula (~3 handfuls)
1 egg yolk
1/4 teaspoon garlic minced
1/4 cup + 2 TB lemon juice freshly squeezed

1 cup + 4 TB extra virgin olive oil
kosher salt to taste
1 pound crabmeat
1 small jalapeño pepper seeded & diced
1 pinch seasoned salt

Separate the endive leaves, then slice them lengthwise as thinly as possible. Soak the sliced endive in a big bowl of ice water. Meanwhile, remove outer leaves of the chicory and reserve for another use. Wash four big handfuls of the tender inner chicory leaves. Tear them into bite-size pieces and add to the bowl of ice water. Wash the arugula and add it to the ice water. Set aside for at least 10 minutes or until ready to use.

Make the aioli. Put egg yolk, garlic and 2 tablespoons lemon juice into the bowl of a food processor and pulse to combine. Slowly emulsify with 1 cup of extra-virgin olive oil. If at any point the aioli becomes superglossy or the oil begins to bead, add a drop of ice water, then continue to stream in the oil. Season with salt to taste. Set aside.

Season crab with 1 TB Aioli, 1/4 cup lemon juice, 2 TB olive oil and 1 tsp kosher salt. Add diced jalapeno. Set aside.

Drain the greens, then spin dry using a salad spinner. Transfer into a large bowl. Scatter about 1/4 cup of the dressed crabmeat on each plate. Place a layer of greens atop the crab and then a little more crab again. Finish each plate with a dollop of aioli on the side and a sprinkle of seasoned salt on top.

Creamy Yogurt Potato Salad

Cook Time: 4 hours chill   Yield: 4 cups
Recipe from Maureen Heritage

1/2 cup mayonnaise
1/2 cup plain yogurt
3 tablespoons cider vinegar
2 tablespoons sugar
1 teaspoon salt + pinch pepper

4 cups cooked potatoes peeled & sliced
1/2 cup green onions
2 stalks celery chopped
2-3 hard boiled eggs sliced

In a large bowl, stir together first 5 ingredients. Add potatoes, onions, celery and eggs. Toss to coat well. Cover and Chill 4 hours. If desired, sprinkle with chopped parsley.

KFC Coleslaw

Recipe from Pat Olds

1 head (~ 8 cups) cabbage chopped
1 medium carrot shredded
2 tablespoons onions minced
1/2 cup mayonnaise
1/4 cup buttermilk

1/3 cup sugar
1 tablespoon white vinegar
1/2 teaspoon salt
1/8 teaspoon pepper

Mix all ingredients together, cover and refrigerate at least 2 hours. Overnight is even better.

Oriental Noodle Salad

Recipe from Kathleen Jusko

2 packages beef flavored ramen soup mix (not low fat)
1 pound pre-chopped raw cabbage coleslaw mix
1 cup sunflower seed unsalted
1 cup toasted, slivered almonds
1 bunch green onions including tops, finely chopped

Dressing
2 tablespoons up to 3/4 cup salad oil
1/2 cup sugar
1/3 cup white vinegar
1 teaspoon onion powder
2 packages of seasoning from ramen noodles
dash salt & pepper

Break uncooked noodles into a large bowl. Toss the other ingredients onto the noodles and mix.

In a separate bowl or jar, make dressing. At least one hour before serving, pour the dressing over the noodles, mixing well. Allow time for noodles to absorb dressing before serving. Refrigerate. Can be made several days ahead.

Roasted Pepper Salad

Recipe from Kathleen Jusko

4 roasted green bell peppers (or any color peppers)
1 bunch cilantro chopped
1 cup Calamata or black olives cut in half
4-6 ounces Fontina or gouda cheese cut into julienne strips

Dressing
2 tablespoons heavy cream
2 tablespoons cider vinegar
1 tablespoon prepared mustard

Mix Roasted Peppers with olives and cheese. Make dressing and spoon dressing over roasted peppers one 1 Tablespoon at a time & toss. Don't overload with dressing.

Salad Dressing for Tomatoes

Recipe from Pat Olds

Use as salad dressing or dip for fresh summer tomatoes

2 eggs
1/4 teaspoon dry mustard
1/2 cup sugar
1 tablespoon flour

1/2 teaspoon salt
1/2 cup malt or cider vinegar
1/2 pint heavy cream

Beat eggs, add mustard, sugar, flour, salt and vinegar. Stir over low heat until thick as pudding. Cool before adding heavy cream.

Kathy Rupff

@2012 Pamela Eden

Pamela Eden

Sliced Tomato Salad
Makes 12 servings

Preparation: 25 minutes
You may also add sliced cucumbers or thinly sliced zucchini for color and variety.

8 large tomatoes cut in 1/4" slices
2 large sweet onions halved & thinly sliced
1/3 cup olive oil
2 tablespoons lemon juice

1 teaspoon oregano
3/4 teaspoon salt
1/4 teaspoon pepper
2 tablespoons fresh parsley minced

Arrange alternating slices of tomatoes and onions on a large rimmed serving platter. In a small bowl, whisk the olive oil, lemon juice, oregano, salt & pepper. Drizzle over tomato and onion slices. Sprinkle with parsley.

Sour Cream Potato Salad

Recipe by Deette Little

2 pounds potatoes peeled, cooked & cubed
1 onion chopped
1 teaspoon salt
1 teaspoon celery seed

1 cup sour cream
1/2 cup mayonnaise
2 tablespoons white wine vinegar
1 teaspoon spicy brown mustard

Put the potatoes and onion in a large bowl. Mix together the next 6 ingredients to make the dressing. Pour over the potatoes and onions. Gently toss the ingredients
Refrigerate until ready to serve.

Summer Potato and Basil Salad

Recipe from Pamela Eden

1 pound baby red potato cleaned & cut into chunks
5 ears corn shucked and cleaned
1 pint grape tomato halved
1 small red onion thinly sliced
1 bunch fresh basil

1/4 cup extra virgin olive oil
2 lemons juiced
2 teaspoons all-purpose greek seasoning
1 (6-ounce) package crumbled Athenos Crumble Traditional Feta Cheese

In separate pots, cook the potatoes and corn. Cook the potatoes in boiling water until they are fork tender- about 10 - 15 minutes. Cook the corn in boiling water for 5-7 minutes until they are tender. When the potatoes and corn are ready, drain the water and submerge them in an ice bath to stop further cooking.

After the potatoes and corn have cooled down, drain them well. Place the potatoes into a bowl. Cut the kernels off each ear of corn and add to the potatoes. Add the grape tomatoes, onion, crumbled feta cheese and whole basil leaves. Drizzle the vegetables with olive oil and lemon juice and toss to coat. Season to taste with Greek seasoning. Serve immediately.

Tabouli

Makes 6 servings

Cook Time: 3 hrs
Recipe from Pamela Eden

1 cup dry bulgur wheat
1 1/2 cups boiling water
1 1/2 teaspoons salt
1/4 cup fresh lemon juice
1 teaspoon crushed garlic
1/2 cup fresh scallion chopped (include greens)
1/2 teaspoon dried mint leaves
1/4 cup good olive oil

1/8 teaspoon pepper
2 medium tomatoes diced
1 cup fresh parsley chopped
1/2 cup cooked garbanzo beans
1 green bell pepper chopped
1 summer squash or cucumber chopped
1/2 cup carrot coarsely grated
1 (6-ounce) package feta cheese crumbled
1/4 cup black olives sliced

You should begin to soak the bulghar at least 3 hours before serving time. It needs to thoroughly marinate and chill.

Combine bulghar, boiling water and salt in a bowl. Cover and let stand 15 -20 minutes or until the bulghar is chewable. Add lemon juice, garlic, oil and mint and mix thoroughly. Refrigerate 2 -3 hours. Just before serving add the vegetables and mix gently. Garnish with feta cheese and olives.

Tomato Soup French Dressing

Makes 4 servings

Recipe by Kathleen Jusko

1 can condensed tomato soup
3/4 cup vinegar
1 teaspoon salt
1/2 teaspoon pepper
1/2 cup sugar

1 teaspoon dry mustard
1 small onion finely chopped (1/4 cup)
1 clove garlic finely minced
1/2 cup vegetable oil

Mix all ingredients with electric mixer till completely blended.

Wheely Good Pasta Salad

Recipe from Marie Gelsomino

1 package (16 oz) wagon wheel pasta (rotelle)
8 ounces Cheddar cheese diced

1 medium red bell pepper diced
2 teaspoons fresh oregano minced
1 bottle cheesy ranch salad dressing

Cook pasta according to package directions, drain and rinse in cold water. In a large serving bowl, combine pasta, cheese, red pepper and oregano. Drizzle with dressing and toss to coat. Cover and refrigerate until ready to serve.

Gordon Perry

Gordon Perry

Gordon Perry

White Bean and Asparagus Salad with Tarragon-Lemon dressing

Preparation: 20 minutes   Yield: 4-6 servings
Recipe from William Reynolds

8 ounces dried white beans or
2 (15-ounce) cans Great Northern or cannelli
   beans
salt
2 bay leaves (if using dried beans)
1 pound asparagus spears

1/2 cup tarragon leaves
1 teaspoon packed lemon zest finely grated
2 cloves garlic peeled
1/4 teaspoon freshly ground black pepper
1 large lemon juiced
1/2 cup olive oil

If using canned beans, drain and rinse.

If using dried beans, soak in plenty of water for 6 hours or overnight. Drain beans and transfer to a medium pot. Cover beans by 2 inches with water and add 1-1/2 teaspoons salt and the bay leaves. Simmer until just tender but not mushy, about 45 minutes to 1-1/2 hours depending on the type of beans you are using. Drain.

Break off tough ends of the asparagus. Bring a medium pot salted water to a boil and prepare a bowl with ice and cold water. Blanch trimmed asparagus for 1-1/2 minutes, or until just cooked through but still firm, then plunge them into the ice bath. Let sit for 5 minutes, then drain. Pat dry and slice diagonally into 1/2 inch pieces.

In a blender or food processor, combine tarragon leaves, lemon zest, garlic, salt, pepper and lemon juice and process until garlic is chopped. Pour in olive oil. Process until mixture is well blended and bright green about 1 minute.

In a large bowl, gently toss together beans, asparagus and dressing. Taste and add more lemon juice and salt if needed.

Patti Tivnan

Chapter 4: Casseroles

3 Cheese Macaroni

Yield: 6 servings

Three kinds of cheese give this a rich flavor and a hearty texture.

8 ounces (2 1/2 cups) macaroni
2 tablespoons butter
2 tablespoons flour
1/2 teaspoon salt
1/2 teaspoon dry mustard
2 cups milk

1/2 cup shredded Cheddar cheese divided
1/2 cup shredded mozzarella cheese divided
1/2 cup shredded Swiss cheese divided
TOPPING
2 tablespoons butter
1/2 cup seasoned bread crumbs

Pre-heat oven to 400F and grease an 11 x 7" baking dish. For the casserole, cook the macaroni according to the package directions. Drain.

Meanwhile, melt butter in a large sauce pan over medium heat. Add the flour and salt. whisk until smooth. Stir in the mustard. Gradually add the milk stirring constantly. Reduce heat to low. cook stirring constantly until thickened, about 5 minutes.

Stir 1/4 cup cheddar, mozzarella and swiss each into the pot. Remove from the heat. In a large bowl, combine the cooked macaroni and cheese mixture. Spoon the macaroni mixture into the prepared baking dish. Sprinkle with the remaining cheeses.

For the topping, place the butter in a microwave safe bowl. Microwave on high util butter is melted, about 15 seconds. Stir in bread crumbs. Mix well. Sprinkle over top of macaroni and cheese. Bake until hot and bubbly about 15 minutes.

Baked Beans Extraordinare

Recipe from Kathleen Jusko

4 (16-ounce) cans baked beans drained
3/4 pound ground beef
1/2 pound ground sausage
1 teaspoon cayenne pepper
3/4 cup molasses
3/4 cup barbecue sauce

8 -10 slices bacon
1 teaspoon Worcestershire sauce
1/2 teaspoon salt
1 1/2 cups onions finely chopped
1/2 teaspoon angostura bitters
1 teaspoon liquid smoke

Mix all ingredients in a large lightly greased casserole dish at 350F for 45 minutes.

Baked Corn Pudding

Recipe from Kathleen Jusko

2 eggs
1/4 cup sugar
12 ounces creamed corn
1 can evaporated milk

1 tablespoon cornstarch
2 pats butter on top before baking
pinch salt

Pre-heat oven to 350F

Beat eggs. Add sugar and milk and mix. Combine corn starch with evaporated milk and creamed corn. Pour into greased 9x9 baking dish. Dot top with a couple pats of butter. Bake 45 minutes.

Baked Ziti with Pumpkin & Sausage

Preparation: 20 mins   Yield: 12 servings

Recipe from Pamela Eden | Source: verybestbaking.com

nonstick cooking spray
4 cups (12 oz.) dry regular or whole-wheat ziti
1 can (15 oz.) libby's® 100% pure pumpkin
2 tablespoons all-purpose flour
1 teaspoon garlic powder
1/2 teaspoon salt
1/4 teaspoon ground nutmeg
pinch cayenne pepper

1 (12-ounce) can evaporated milk
4 links (12 oz.) fully-cooked italian-seasoned chicken sausages, cut into 1/4-inch slices
1 package (6 oz.) or about 4 cups pre-washed baby spinach
1 cup (4 oz.) shredded part-skim or 2% milk reduced-fat mozzarella cheese
1/2 cup (1.5 oz.) shredded Parmesan cheese

PREHEAT oven to 425º F. Spray 4-quart baking dish with nonstick cooking spray.

PREPARE pasta according to package directions. Reserve 1/2 cup pasta cooking water and set aside for later use. Drain pasta; return to cooking pot. COMBINE pumpkin, flour, garlic powder, salt, nutmeg and cayenne pepper in medium skillet over medium heat. Slowly add evaporated milk, stirring until smooth. Cook, stirring occasionally, for 2 to 3 minutes or until mixture begins to thicken slightly. Pour over pasta in pot. Add sausage and reserved pasta cooking water; stir well. SPREAD half of the pasta mixture into prepared baking dish. Top with spinach. Cover with remaining pasta mixture. Lightly spray piece of foil with nonstick cooking spray. Cover ziti with foil, greased side down. BAKE for 20 minutes or until heated through.

Combine mozzarella and Parmesan cheeses in small bowl. Remove foil; sprinkle with cheese mixture. Bake, uncovered, for an additional 5 minutes or until cheese is melted.

Broccoli Corn Casserole

Cook Time: 30 minutes
Recipe from Ruth Grabner

1 package chopped broccoli thawed, uncooked
1 egg beaten

1 can cream style corn
1 1/2 cups Pepperidge Farm Stuffing
1/2 stick butter melted

Pre-heat oven to 350. Mix stuffing mix with melted butter. Mix broccoli, egg and corn together with 1 cup of stuffing mix in a casserole and sprinkle remainder of mix on top.

Bake for 30 minutes.

Corn Custard

Makes 6 servings

Recipe from Maureen Heritage

2 eggs
1 cup yellow sweet corn
1/2 cup fine cracker crumbs
2 tablespoons sugar

3/4 teaspoon salt
2 cups milk
1 tablespoon butter melted

Beat eggs and add the other ingredients in order listed. Pour into a greased casserole or baking dish and bake about 1 hour in a very slow oven (325F). Casserole may be placed in a pan of hot water while baking. Serve hot. To vary the flavor, add 1/4 C grated cheese.

Creamy Carrot Casserole

Cook Time: 30 minutes
Recipe from Ruth Grabner

Yield: 8 -10 servings

1 1/2 pounds carrots peeled & sliced
1 cup mayonnaise
1 tablespoon onion grated
Pre-heat oven to 350F

1 tablespoon horseradish
1/4 cup shredded Cheddar cheese
2 tablespoons buttered bread crumbs

In saucepan, cook carrots till crisp tender. Drain and reserve 1/4Cup liquid. Place carrots in 1 1/2 Qt baking dish. Combine mayo, onion, horseradish and reserved carrot liquid. Spread evenly over carrots. Sprinkle with cheese, top with bread crumbs. Bake uncovered for 30 minutes.

Franks Hawaiianaise

Recipe from Maureen Heritage

2 tablespoons cornstarch
1/2 cup packed brown sugar
2 teaspoons soy sauce
1/3 cup cider vinegar

1 (20-ounce) can pineapple chunks
1 pound hot dog
2 green peppers

In a large skillet combine Cornstarch, brown sugar, soy sauce, vinegar and liquid drained from pineapple chunks. Stir and cook over medium heat until thickened. Add hotdogs (scored or cut in thirds), pineapple chunks and 2 green peppers which have been cut into 1 inch chunks.

If desired, add sweet red peppers, maraschino cherries or tomato wedges. Heat & Serve over hot fluffy rice.

Patti Tivnan

Huspot

Cook Time: 1 hour
Recipe from Carol Southerland

1 pound ground beef
onion flakes
Italian seasoning
salt

pepper
6 potatoes sliced thin
1 can sliced carrot drained
1 can tomato sauce

Brown ground beef in frying pan. Drain off fat. Season to taste with seasonings. Add potatoes and drained carrots. Stir to mix well. Cook till warmed through.

If using a frying pan that can go in the oven at 350F, otherwise transfer to a greased casserole dish and cover with tomato sauce. Bake 1 - 1.5 hours until potatoes are done.

Irene's Green Bean

Cook Time: 30 minutes
Recipe from Kathleen Jusko

1 large sweet onion cut in wedges
1/4 cup olive oil
3 tablespoons packed brown sugar
2 pounds fresh green beans cooked
6 ounces baby mushrooms
Pre-heat oven to 400F

2 tablespoons olive oil
6 ounces goat cheese
1 tablespoon soy sauce
2 teaspoons balsamic vinegar
2 tablespoons milk

Cook onion till carmelized in oil (covered). Uncover onion and add brown sugar and continue carmelizing. set aside. In 3 Qt baking dish, put beans, add mushrooms, combine oil, soy sauce and vinegar. Pour over beans. Toss to coat. Bake `15-20 minutes. Combine cheese and milk. Spoon this mix along the length down the center of the beans. Top with onions. Return to oven another 8 -10 minutes.

Mom's Macaroni and Cheese

Cook Time: 30 minutes
Recipe from Marie Gelsomino

(tasteofhome.com)

1-1/2 cup uncooked elbow Macaroni
7 tablespoons butter divided
4-1/2 tablespoons flour
2-1/4 cups milk
1-1/3 cup shredded Cheddar cheese

3 ounces processed American cheese cubed
3/4 teaspoon salt
1/4 teaspoon pepper
2 tablespoons dry bread crumbs

Cook macaroni according to package directions, drain. Place in a greased 1-1/2 qt baking dish and set aside. In a saucepan, melt 6 TB butter over medium heat. Stir in flour until smooth. Gradually add milk; bring to a boil. Cook and stir for 2 minutes, reduce heat. Stir in cheeses, salt, pepper until the cheese is melted. Pour over macaroni, mix well. Melt the remaining butter, add the bread crumbs. Sprinkle over casserole. Bake uncovered, at 375F for 30 minutes.

Mushroom Casserole

Cook Time: 55 minutes
Recipe from Kathleen Jusko

1 pound mushrooms
3 cubes chicken bouillon
4 tablespoons flour
1/2 teaspoon pepper

1 cup sour cream
2 tablespoons grated Parmesan cheese
2 cups seasoned stuffing mix
1 cup butter melted

Mix chicken bullion cubes, flour, pepper, sour cream and parmesan cheese and pour over mushrooms. Mix stuffing and melted butter to be sure stuffing is thoroughly coated with butter. Bake all in a covered casserole dish at 350F for 55 minutes.

Nana's Potatoes

Cook Time: 30 minutes.
Recipe from Kathleen Jusko

6 medium potatoes cooked & grated
1 pint sour cream
10 ounces Cheddar cheese grated
1/2 - 1 cup onion grated
3 tablespoons milk

1 teaspoon salt
1/4 teaspoon pepper
2 tablespoons butter melted
1/2 cup bread crumbs

Pre-heat oven to 350F. Grease 9x13 pan. Mix together melted butter and bread crumbs - set aside. Combine all remaining ingredients and spread in greased pan. Top with breadcrumb mixture. Bake 30 minutes.

Potato Casserole

Cook Time: 45 minutes
Yield: 6 servings
Recipe from Pat Olds

6 medium potatoes
1/4 cup butter
1 can cream of chicken soup
1/2 pint (8 oz) sour cream

1/3 cup chopped green onions
1 1/2 cups shredded Cheddar cheese
1 cup crushed cornflakes mixed w/2 TB melted butter

Cook potatoes until tender. Cool, peel and grate or rice them. Heat 1/4c butter with soup, blend in sour cream, onion and cheese into the soup. Stir in the potatoes and place in buttered 2 1/2 QT casserole dish. Mix cornflakes with melted butter and layer over top of casserole. Bake at 350F for 45 minutes.

Ruth's Chicken Casserole

Cook Time: 1.5 hours
Recipe from Ruth Grabner

4 chicken breasts boned and split
6 slices Swiss cheese
1/2 cup wine or chicken broth

1/4 pound margarine melted
1 can cream of chicken soup
2 cups Pepperidge Farm Stuffing

Place chicken in 9 x 13 dish and cover with cheese. Mix soup with wine and pour over chicken. Mix Stuffing with melted butter and spread out over top. Bake 1.5 hours at 300F.

Scalloped Potatoes

Recipe from Marie Gelsomino

6-8 potatoes
1/2 medium onion sliced 1/4" thick
1-1/2 cup milk
1/3 cup flour

dash salt
dash pepper
4 tablespoons butter softened

Peel and slice potatoes 1/4" thick. Slice onions 1/4" thick. Make 2-3 layers alternating potatoes and onions in a casserole dish. Sprinkle flour, salt and pepper on each layer. Dot with butter on each layer. Pour milk over potatoes. Bake at 350F for 1-1/4 hours or until potatoes are tender and browned on top.

Slow Cooker Mac-n-Cheese

Cook Time: 4 hours   Yield: 10 servings
This recipe is great to take to a pot luck since it makes a considerable quantity.

1 package (16 oz) elbow Macaroni
1/2 cup butter melted
2 eggs beaten
1 can (12 oz) evaporated milk
1 can (10 3/4 oz) condensed chedder cheese soup

1 cup milk
4 cups (16 oz) Cheddar cheese shredded, divided
1/8 teaspoon paprika

Cook macaroni according to package directions; drain. Place in a 5 qt slow cooker. Add butter. In a bowl, combine the eggs, evaporated milk, soup, milk and 3 cups cheese. Pour over macaroni mixture. Stir to combine. Cover and cook on low for 4 hours. Sprinkle with the remaining cheese. Cook 15 minutes longer or until cheese is melted. Sprinkle with paprika.

Sweet Potato Bake

Recipe from Kathleen Jusko

6 medium sweet potatoes peeled
10 tablespoons unsalted butter melted

1 tablespoon fresh thyme (or 1 tsp dried)
Coarse sea salt and ground pepper

Pre heat oven to 425F. Using a mandoline or sharp knife, slice potatoes about 1/8 inch thick. Place in a very large bowl, add butter, thyme, salt & pepper. Toss well until all slices are well coated. Reserve about a dozen of the best looking slices for top layer. Arrange a layer of slightly overlapping slices in 10" round grain dish, skillet or other shallow oven proof dish. Layer potatoes until all are used, topping with reserved potatoes.

Place a sheet of heavy duty foil directly on top of potatoes. Place pan in oven, and place a heavy pan slightly smaller directly on top of the foil. Bake for 30 minutes. Remove top pan and carefully peel away foil. Continue baking until potatoes are soft and top is almost carmalized, 20 -30 minutes longer. Cut into wedges and serve hot.

Tomato Crouton Casserole

Cook Time: 30 minutes
Recipe by Kathleen Jusko

1 (28-ounce) can diced tomato undrained
2 cups stuffing croutons seasoned
1 small onion chopped
1 tablespoon sugar
Pre-heat oven to 375F

1/4 teaspoon dried oregano
1/4 teaspoon salt
1/8 teaspoon pepper
3 tablespoons butter (or margarine)

In a greased 2 qt casserole, mix tomatoes and 1 cup of croutons. Stir in onions, sugar, oregano, salt & pepper. Dot with butter. Top with remaining croutons.
Bake for 30- 35 minutes

Tomato Nacho Casserole

Cook Time: 30 minutes
Recipe by Kathleen Jusko

1/2 cup fine chopped onion
1 clove minced garlic
2 tablespoons margarine
1 cup sour cream
12 plum tomatoes
Pre-heat oven to 350F

1/4 teaspoon pepper
2 cups shredded Cheddar cheese
1 1/2 bags crushed tortilla chips or nacho chips

In a small skillet saute onion and garlic in butter until tender. Stir in sour cream. Place tomatoes in 12x8 inch buttered baking dish. Sprinkle with pepper and cheese.
Spread sour cream over cheese. Sprinkle with crushed corn chips. Bake for 25 minutes.

Yam Bake

Cook Time: 30 minutes
Recipe from Kathleen Jusko

2/3 cup evaporated milk
1 cup old fashioned rolled oats
1 (18-ounce) can yam cooked & mashed
1 (8 3/4-ounce) can crushed pineapple chunks drained

1/2 cup packed brown sugar
2 tablespoons butter
1 egg
1 teaspoon vanilla extract

Pre-heat oven to 400F. Grease 1 1/2 qt baking dish. Pour milk over oats and let stand for 5 mintues. Mix well with remaining ingredients. Pour into a greased baking dish and bake for 30 minutes.

Variations: just before baking swirl in 1/2 cup whole berry cranberry sauce or 1/2 cup marshmallow cream.

Chapter 5: Soups, Chowders, Stews, Sauces

Ruth Grabner

Cheesy Vegetable Soup

Cook Time: 20 minutes
Yield: 4 servings
Recipe from Kathleen Jusko

2 tablespoons onions chopped
1 tablespoon butter or margarine
1 cup frozen corn
1/2 cup frozen broccoli chopped
1/4 cup shredded carrot
1/4 cup water

1 (10 3/4-ounce) can condensed cream of
 potato soup
1 cup milk
1/4 cup shredded Cheddar cheese
1 ounce provolone cheese cut up
dash pepper

In a medium saucepan cook onion in hot margarine or butter until tender but not brown. Add corn, broccoli, carrots and water. Bring to a boil. Reduce heat and cover to simmer for 10 minutes or until veggies are tender. Stir in condensed soup, milk, cheeses and pepper. Cook and stir over medium heat until cheeses are melted and mixture is heated through.

Chicken & Vegetable Stew

Recipe from Kathleen Jusko

4 -6 chicken thighs
1 clove garlic minced
1 medium onion chopped
2 -4 carrots sliced diagnoally 1" thick
1-2 small zucchini thick slices
3-4 large potatoes chopped

4 ounces mushrooms thick slices
1 1/2 cups water
1 ounce Knorr's Chicken Stock
1/2 - 1 teaspoon marjoram
salt & pepper to taste

Saute Chicken in olive oil. After turning, add onion, garlic and carrots. Sprinkle with salt & pepper, add water and chicken broth. Cover with lid, turn heat to medium and cook 15 minutes. Add potatoes, zucchini, mushrooms - cover and simmer for another 15 minutes or until potatoes are cooked through. Give it a good stir,then pull contents to one side of the pot and thicken the juices (stir 1 Tablespoon flour into 1/4 cup water) stir into juices till thickened. Recombine all ingredients in pot.

Chicken and Dumpling Soup

Makes 4 servings

Preparation: 25 minutes, Cook Time: 40 minutes
Source: TasteofHome.com - Sept/Oct 2013

3/4 pound boneless, skinless chicken breast
 cut into cubes
1/4 teaspoon salt
1/8 teaspoon pepper
2 teaspoons olive oil
1/4 cup flour
4 cups reduced-sodium chicken broth divided
1 cup water
2 cups frozen French cut green beans

1-1/2 cup sliced onion
1 cup shredded carrot
1/4 teaspoon marjoram
2/3 cup Reduced-Fat Bisquick® baking mix
1/3 cup cornmeal
1/4 cup shredded reduced-fat Cheddar
 cheese
1/3 cup fat-free milk

Sprinkle chicken with salt and pepper. In a large non-stick skillet heat oil over medium high heat. Add chicken, cook and stir until no longer pink. Remove from heat. In a large saucepan, whisk flour and 1/2 cup broth until smooth. Stir in water and remaining broth. Add beans, onion,carrots and marjoram. Bring to a boil. Reduce heat, simmer uncovered 10 minutes. Add chicken, return to simmer. Meanwhile, in a small bowl, mix biscuit mix, cornmeal and cheese. Stir in milk just until moistened. Drop batter in 12 portions on top of the simmering soup. Reduce heat to low, cover and cook 15 minutes or until a toothpick inserted in the center of dumpling comes out clean.

Chicken Potpie Recipe

Preparation: 40 minutes, Cook Time: 35 minutes

Source: tasteofhome.com

2 cups diced peeled potatoes
1-3/4 cup sliced carrot
1 cup butter, cubed
2/3 cup chopped onion
1 cup all-purpose flour
1-3/4 teaspoon salt
1 teaspoon dried thyme

3/4 teaspoon pepper
3 cups chicken broth
1-1/2 cup milk
4 cups cubed cooked chicken
1 cup frozen peas
1 cup frozen corn
2 packages refrigerated pie crust

Preheat oven to 425°. Place potatoes and carrots in a large saucepan; add water to cover. Bring to a boil. Reduce heat; cook, covered, 8-10 minutes or until vegetables are crisp-tender; drain. In a large skillet, heat butter over medium-high heat. Add onion; cook and stir until tender. Stir in flour and seasonings until blended. Gradually stir in broth and milk. Bring to a boil, stirring constantly; cook and stir 2 minutes or until thickened. Stir in chicken, peas, corn and potato mixture; remove from heat. Unroll a pastry sheet into each of two 9-in. pie plates; trim even with rims. Add chicken mixture. Unroll remaining pastry; place over filling. Trim, seal and flute edges. Cut slits in tops. Bake 35-40 minutes or until crust is lightly browned. Let stand 15 minutes before cutting. Yield: 2 potpies (8 servings each).

Freeze option: Cover and freeze unbaked pies. To use, remove from freezer 30 minutes before baking (do not thaw). Preheat oven to 425°. Place pies on baking sheets; cover edges loosely with foil. Bake 30 minutes. Reduce oven setting to 350°; bake 70-80 minutes longer or until crust is golden brown and a thermometer inserted in center reads 165°.

Kathy Rupff

Kathy Rupff

SHEEP

Pamela Eden

Chipotle Butternut Squash Soup

Yield: 12 servings

Recipe from Pat Olds

2 cups diced, peeled butternut squash
1 small carrot finely chopped
1 green onion sliced
1/2 teaspoon cumin
1 tablespoon olive oil
2 cloves garlic minced
2 cups vegetable broth
1 (14 1/2-ounce) can diced tomatoes
    undrained

1 package (3 oz) cream cheese cubed
1/4 cup fresh basil minced
1 chopped chipotle chili in adobo sauce
1 (15 1/2-ounce) can black beans rinsed &
    drained
1 (11-ounce) can Mexicorn drained
2 cups fresh baby spinach chopped

In a large sauce pan, saute the squash, carrot, onion & cumin i oil for 10 minutes. Add garlic, cook 1 minute longer. Add 1-1/2s cu broth, bring to a boil. reduce heat. Cover and simmer for 10-12 minutes or until vegetables are tender. Cool slightly. Transfer mixture to a blender, add the tomatoes, cream cheese, basil, chipotle pepper and the remaining broth. Cover and process for 1-2 minutes or until smooth. Return to saucepan, stir in the beans, corn and spinach. Cook and stir until spinach is wilted and soup is heated through.

Corn Chowder Gelsomino

Recipe from Marie Gelsomino

5 tablespoons butter
1/3 cup flour
1 quart water
1 quart milk

1 bag (2 lbs) frozen cut   corn or
    4-5 ears fresh
1 medium onion chopped
1 stalk celery
2 medium carrots diced

Saute vegetables in butter until tender. Stir in flour. Add water, milk, and corn kernels and boil 10 minutes. Simmer until corn is tender. Stir frequently, skim off foam

If using fresh corn, cut kernels off cob and scrape remainder from corn with the back of a knife for richer flavor.

Corn Chowder Supreme

Recipe by Kathleen Jusko

1 cup chopped carrot
4 small onions chopped
2 tablespoons butter
1 (8-ounce) can creamed corn yellow
1 cup condensed cream of mushroom soup

2 cups milk
1/2 teaspoon salt
1/8 teaspoon pepper
2 slices crisp bacon

Cook carrots until tender in water. In soup pot cook back till crisp, set aside. In same pot cook onions in butter till golden. Add back bacon and remaining ingredients. Heat throughly without boiling.

Kathleen Jusko

Cream of Broccoli Soup

Recipe by Marie Gelsomino

1 head broccoli
4 cups milk
1 1/2 cups water
4 tablespoons butter

4 tablespoons flour
dash salt
dash pepper

Cut broccoli into florets and rinse in cold water. Combine milk and water and bring to boil. Add broccoli and cook until tender. In small pot, melt butter and stir in flour. Whisk for 2 minutes over low heat, stirring until lump-free. Pour sauce slowly into broccoli pot stirring constantly until smooth. Add salt and pepper to taste.

Note: Potato Flakes or mashed potatoes may be added if soup seems too thin.

Gaspacho

Recipe from Pat Olds

This is a cold fresh vegetable soup. Perfect for hot summer days.

2 ounces onions
1 green bell pepper
1 cucumber
1 tomato
1 clove garlic minced
1/2 teaspoon salt & pepper
1 pinch cayenne pepper
1 pinch thyme

1 pinch summer savory
1 tablespoon tomato paste
1/8 cup white wine vinegar
1/8 cup olive oil
1/2 ounce lemon juice
1 raw egg
3/4 cup tomato juice

Place all ingredients except tomato juice in blender a little at a time and when they are all mixed, add the tomato juice.

Refrigerate in a covered glass container until well chilled.

You may want to garnish it with additional diced tomatoes, cucumber, onions and green peppers. You can also add zucchini and celery or season with Tabasco sauce.

Italian Green Bean Stew

Recipe by Marie Gelsomino

1 jar spaghetti sauce
1 pound boneless beef chuck cubed
6-8 potatoes peeled & cubed

1/2 bag frozen italian green bean (or 1 can of Italian green beans)
1 cup water

Brown beef in oil in a Dutch oven. Drain off fat and add tomato sauce. Cook until sauce bubbles. Add 1 (spaghetti jar full) of water and bring to a boil. Peel and cube potatoes before adding to sauce. Boil until potatoes are cooked, then add green beans. Continue to cook until beans are tender.

Jean's Sweet Cheech and Veggie Slow Cooker Stew

Makes 3 servings

Recipe from Jeanmarie Rose Perry

1 (28-ounce) can Italian diced tomatoes
1/2 package baby carrots
1/2 sweet onion sliced
1/2 package dried apricot
2 boneless, skinless chicken breasts

1/4 cup fresh basil
1 can string green beans drained
1/2 cup lowfat cream
1 bag noodles

Add tomatoes, carrots, onion, apricots & chicken to slow cooker. Cover and cook on high for 5 hours or until chicken is cooked. Add basil, beans and cream. Stir to mix ingredients. Cook 1 more hour. Serve with cooked noodles (any type).

Leek Soup

Recipe by Kathleen Jusko

6 leeks cleaned & drained thoughly
3 tablespoons butter or oil or bacon drippings
2 medium potatoes peeled & diced
3 cups chicken broth

1 cup water
1/4 teaspoon nutmeg
1 teaspoon lemon juice
sour cream (or half - half)

Thinly slice leeks in soup pot. Stir in bacon till soft- do not brown. Add in potatoes, broth and water. Simmer 20 -30 minutes til leeks and potatoes are soft. Cool before pureeing and adding nutmeg and lemon juice. Add sour cream or half-half to your liking

Lentil Soup with Sausage and Kale

Cook Time: 40 minutes
Yield: 4 servings
Recipe from Pat Olds

This is one of the "Yum-o!" recipes- it's good and good for you. To find out more about Yum-o!, Rachel's non-profit organization, go to www.yum-o.org

1 tablespoon extra virgin olive oil
1 pound bulk turkey or pork sausage regular
  or hot
1 cup lentils
1 medium onion chopped
3-4 cloves garlic grated or chopped
1/2 pound crimini mushrooms thinly sliced

1 baking potato peeled & diced
2 sprigs rosemary leaves chopped
3-4 sprigs thyme leaves
dash salt & pepper
1/4 cup tomato paste
4 cups chicken broth
1 bunch kale thick stems removed

Place a large soup pot over medium-high heat with one turn of the pan of Extra Virgin Olive oil, ~1 TB. Once hot, add the sausage and saute for 3 -4minutes, breaking it up into small pieces with the back of a spoon or a potato masher as it cooks and browns. While the sausage is browning, pour the lentils out onto a light colored plate and sift through them. Discard any small stones- sometimes you find them and sometimes you don't. Better safe than sorry.

To the browned sausage add the onion, garlic, mushrooms, potato, rosemary, thyme, salt & pepper and tomato paste. Cook, stirring frequently for 3-4 minutes. Add the stock and 2 cups of water. Turn the heat up to high and bring to a boil. Add the lentils and the shredded leaves of the kale. Stir until the kale wilts and the turn the heat down to medium and simmer for 30 -40 minutes until the lentils are tender. Serve.

Meatball Stew

Recipe from Marie Gelsomino

1 pound ground beef
1 jar spaghetti sauce
3/4 cup bread crumbs soaked in hot water
Romano cheese for flavor

2 eggs
5-6 medium potatoes cut into 1" cubes
4-6 carrots
1 bag frozen peas

Mix ground beef, cheese and soaked bread crumbs. Roll into meatballs about 3/4". Fry meatballs in oil until browned using dutch oven. Drain, leaving dripping in pan. Add tomato sauce. Bring to a boil, add water. Peel carrots and potatoes. Cut potatoes into 1" cubes, slice carrots. Add carrots and potatoes to soup, boil until vegetables are tender. Add peas, cook until peas are tender. Serve with Italian bread.

Moroccan Chicken Stew

Preparation: 10 minutes, Cook Time: 40 minutes   Yield: 4

Recipe from Pamela Eden |
Source: campbellskitchen.com

What makes this mouthwatering stew Moroccan? It's the perfect blend of sweet and savory spices, mixed with raisins, chickpeas and almonds. It's so different and so delicious!

- 2 tablespoons olive oil
- 8 skinless, bone-in chicken thighs (about 2 pounds)
- 2 medium red onions, sliced (about 2 cups)
- 1 large green pepper, cut into 1-inch pieces (about 1 1/2 cups)
- 2 cloves garlic, finely chopped
- 1 teaspoon ground cinnamon
- 1 tablespoon curry powder
- 1 can (10 3/4 ounces) campbell's® condensed tomato soup
- 1/3 cup golden raisins
- 1 can (about 15 ounces) chickpeas (garbanzo beans), rinsed and drained
- 1/3 cup slivered almonds, toasted

Heat the oil in a 5-quart saucepot over medium high heat. Add the chicken in batches and cook until well browned on both sides. Remove the chicken from the saucepot. Reduce the heat to medium. Add the onions, pepper and garlic and cook for 5 minutes or until they're tender-crisp. Add the cinnamon and curry and cook and stir for 1 minute. Stir in the soup and heat to a boil. Return the chicken to the saucepot. Reduce the heat to low. Cover and cook for 15 minutes.   Stir the raisins and chickpeas in the saucepot. Cook for 10 minutes or until the chicken is cooked through. Stir in the almonds.

© 2013 Jody Cooke

Pesto Sauce

Recipe by Kathleen Jusko

Great for in soups or over pasta

1/4 cup soft butter
1/4 cup Parmesan cheese
1/2 cup fine chop parsley
1 clove crushed garlic

1 teaspoon dried basil
1/2 teaspoon dried marjoram or Oregano
1/4 cup salad oil or Olive Oil
1/4 cup pine nuts (optional)

With electric mixer, blend 1st 6 ingredients. With better running, gradually add oil. Add pine nuts.

Ratatouille

Recipe from Jeanmarie Rose Perry

2 1/2 cups zucchini sliced
1 medium eggplant cubed
1 cup green pepper diced
1 sweet onion chopped

5 medium tomatoes peeled and diced
1/4 cup canola oil
1 clove garlic crushed
dash salt & pepper

Combine all ingredients in a large frying pan. Cover and heat for approx 15 minutes, stirring occasionally until all are tender.

Red Pepper Dip

Cook Time: 1 hr
Recipe from Pat Olds

12 large red bell peppers   **3 cups sugar**
2 cups apple cider vinegar   **1 tablespoon salt**

In the fall when red peppers are in season… Core & quarter peppers . Pour 1 Cup vinegar into blender & add a few pepper quarters, chop fine then add more peppers until ½ the total peppers are chopped. Pour into large kettle,and repeat process until all peppers are chopped. Add sugar & salt to kettle. Bring to boil & simmer until thickish, about 45 minutes to 1 hour. Spoon into round hamburger freezer set & freeze.

Use as needed over cream cheese during the year. (Pepper mixture will thaw as a block of cream cheese softens.)

Shellfish Minestrone with Basil Pesto

Yield: 4 -6 main servings

Recipe from William Reynolds

For the Pesto   **pinch saffron**
2 ounces fresh basil leaves large fistful   **8 cloves garlic minced**
1 ounce Italian parsley leaves small handful   **1 bay leaf**
2 cloves garlic roughly chopped   **1 bundle fresh thyme sprigs**
salt & pepper   **1 cup tomato chopped**
1/2 cup olive oil   **1 cup cooked cannelli beans**
For Minestrone   **24 Little Neck clams well rinsed**
2 tablespoons olive oil   **7 cups hot fish or chicken broth**
1 large onion diced ~2 cups   **1 pound squid cut in 1/2" rings**
1/2 cup celery diced   **1 cup small green peas**
1/2 cup carrot diced   **1 cup blanched & peeled fava beans**
salt & pepper   **(optional)**
pinch red pepper flakes

Make basil pesto: Put basil, parsley and 2 chopped garlic cloves in a blender. Season lightly with salt and pepper. Add 1/2 cup olive oil and puree on high speed,scraping down sides as necessary. pour into a small serving bowl, cover tightly and set aside.

Make the soup: Put 2 Tablespoons olive oil in a large heavy pot over medium heat. Add onion, celery and carrot, season generously with salt and pepper and stir to coat. Cook for about 2 minutes, until softened. Add red pepper, saffron, 8 cloves minced garlic, bay leaf and thyme and let sizzle, then add tomato and simmer a few minutes more.   Stir in cannellini beans. Add clams, in one layer if possible and 1 cup water. Turn heat to high and put on lid. Keep at a rapid simmer until all clams have opened about 5 minutes. (If desired, remove clams, shuck them and return shucked clams to pot). Add fish stock and bring to simmer. Taste broth and adjust seasoning.

Just before serving, add squid, peas and fava beans (if desired). Simmer for 2 minutes. Ladle into shallow soup bowls and stir 2 teaspoons basil puree into each bowl.

Smoky Black Bean Soup with Chicken Sausage

Yield: 4 servings

Recipe and photo from Kathy Rupff (source: Fitness Magazine)

- 1 teaspoon olive oil
- 1 piece 3 oz link precooked spicy chicken sausage thinly sliced
- 1 large onion finely chopped
- 1 red bell pepper seeded and diced
- 4 cloves garlic minced
- 1 teaspoon ground cumin
- 1/2 teaspoon dried oregano
- 1 (15-ounce) can black beans rinsed and drained

- 2 cups reduced sodium chicken broth
- 1 canned chipotle chili in adobo sauce minced
- 1/3 cup reduced fat sour cream
- 1/2 teaspoon finely grated lime zest
- 4 teaspoons freshly squeezed lime juice
- 1/4 teaspoon honey
- salt

Heat oil in a medium saucepan over medium heat. Add sausage in a single layer, cook until lightly browned. About 2 minutes. Turn and cook 1 minute more. Transfer to a plate lined with paper towels. Add onion and bell pepper to pan; saute until soft. 3 -4 minutes. Add garlic, cumin and oregano. Saute 1 minute more. Stir in beans, broth and chipotle. Bring to a boil. Reduce heat to medium low and simmer 5 minutes. Meanwhile - combine sour cream, lime zest, 1 tsp lime juice and honey in a small bowl. Transfer 1 1/2 cups of soup to a blender and puree. Stir puree back into the soup, add sausage. Stir in remaining lime juice and season with salt to taste. Serve and top with lime flavored sour cream.

Spiked Cucumber Soup

Makes 4 servings

Preparation: 15 minutes
Recipe from William Reynolds

2 peeled, seeded cucumbers chopped
4 peeled, seeded cucumber spears for garnish
1/2 ripe Hass avocado peeled, chopped

2 limes juiced
1 cup Hendrick's gin-
pinch salt

Place all ingredients except the cucumber spears in a blender and process until smooth. Transfer to a large cocktail shaker, shake with ice, then strain into 4 wine goblets (this can be done in two batches if necessary). Garnish each with a cucumber spear.

Sweet & Sour Stew

Cook Time: 2 hours
Recipe by Deette Little

1 1/2 - 2 pounds beef stew meat cubed
1 cup carrot sliced
1 onion sliced
1 (8-ounce) can tomato sauce
1/4 cup white wine vinegar or red wine vinegar

1/4 cup dark brown sugar
1 tablespoon Worcestershire sauce
1/2 cup water
1 package egg noodles cooked per package

Note- An electric frying pan works great for this. Brown beef in frying pan sprayed with non-stick cooking spray. Add the remaining ingredients and simmer till meat is tender about 2 hours. Serve over egg noodles.

Veal Stew with Potatoes, Tomatoes and Oregano

Recipe from William Reynolds

1/4 cup olive oil
2 pounds veal stew meat cut into 1"cubes
16 boiling onions peeled
1-1/4 pound large red-skinned potato peeled

2 tablespoons chopped fresh oregano or
1 tablespoon dried oregano
2 (12-ounce) packages cherry tomatoes halved

Pre-heat oven to 350F. Heat oil in heavy large pot over medium-high heat. Sprinkle veal generously with salt and pepper. Add veal and onions to pot. Saute until veal is no longer pink, about 8 minutes. Mix in potatoes and oregano, then tomatoes. Bring stew to simmer. Cover pot and transfer to oven. Bake until veal and vegetables are tender, about 2 hours. Season stew to taste with salt and pepper. Ladle stew into shallow soup bowls and serve.

West African Beef Stew

Cook Time: 2 hours
Recipe from Pamela Eden | Source: Joy of Cooking

**2 pounds boneless stewing beef cut into 1"
  cubes**
4 tablespoons hot butter or other fat
1 cup onion chopped
2 tablespoons flour

3 tablespoons curry powder
1/4 cup peanut butter (creamy or crunchy)
1 cup water
1 cup coconut milk (or 2 cups beef broth)
1/4 cup golden raisins

In a Dutch oven, brown beef in hot butter. Remove meat from pot and set aside. Add onions to the pot and cook till golden in color. Add flour, curry and peanut butter. Cook for 1 minute with stirring. Slowly add coconut milk and water to the onion spice mixture and stir until thickened. Return the meat and simmer covered about 2 hours or until tender. 20 minutes before the end of the cook time, add raisins.

Serve with Jasmine rice (made with coconut milk & water) or coucous.

Patti Tivnan

Chapter 6: Entrees

Meat: BBQ Pot Roast

Makes 6 servings

Preparation: 40 minutes, Cook Time: 4 hours
Recipe by Kathleen Jusko

2 teaspoons salt
1/4 teaspoon pepper
3 pounds beef chuck roast
3 tablespoons vegetable oil
1 (8-ounce) can tomato sauce
1 cup water
3 medium onions sliced

2 cloves minced garlic
1/4 cup lemon juice
1/4 cup ketchup
2 tablespoons brown sugar
1 tablespoon Worcestershire sauce
1/2 teaspoon dry mustard

Combine salt & pepper. Rub over roast. Heat oil in dutch oven, brown roast on all sides. Add the tomato sauce, water, onions, garlic. Cover & Simmer for 30 minutes.
Combine remaining ingredients and pour over meat. Cover & Simmer for 3 -4 hours until meat is tender.

Meat: Crockpot Beef and Potatoes with Rosemary

Cook Time: 8 hrs
Recipe from William Reynolds

3 pounds boneless beef chuck roast
1 pound medium red potato cut in fourths
1 cup baby carrot
3 tablespoons Dijon style mustard
2 tablespoons fresh or 1 1/2 tsp dried
    rosemary chopped / crumbled

1 teaspoon fresh or 1/2 tsp dried thyme
1 teaspoon salt
1/2 teaspoon pepper
1 small onion chopped
1 1/2 cups beef broth

Arrange potatoes and carrots around outer edge in 4- to 6-quart slow cooker. Mix mustard, rosemary, thyme, salt and pepper in small bowl; spread evenly over beef. Place beef in slow cooker (it will overlap vegetables slightly). Sprinkle onion over meat. Pour broth evenly over meat and vegetables. Cover and cook on Low heat setting 8 to 9 hours.   Remove meat and vegetables from cooker, using slotted spoon. Place meat on cutting board and slice.

Serve over rice or noodles.

Meat: Kielbasa and Sauerkraut - Gluten Free

Recipe from Merle Morse

1 pound kielbasa cut into 1" thick slices
1 large onion chopped
1 (16-ounce) can potato drained, rinsed &
    sliced

1 (16-ounce) can sauerkraut
1 teaspoon celery seed
1 teaspoon caraway
1/4 teaspoon garlic powder

In a Dutch Oven, Saute onion until tender. Add Kielbasa, potatoes and sauerkraut. Stir. Add celery, caraway and garlic powder. Stir together and cook over low heat 5 -10 minutes until warmed throughout.

Kathy Rupff

Meat: Maple Pork and Apples

Cook Time: 20 Minutes

Recipe by Pamela Eden | Source: recipe.com

Apples and pork play well together in this everyday easy meal. Even with the addition of carrots this quick dinner is done in 20 minutes.

4 pork loin chops, cut 1/2-inch thick (about 1-3/4 lb.)
salt and ground black pepper
2 tbsp. butter

12 baby carrots with tops, halved lengthwise
1 medium apple sliced and seeds removed
1/3 cup pure maple syrup

Sprinkle chops with salt and pepper. In skillet melt butter over medium heat; add chops. Brown for 2 minutes, turning once. Reduce heat to medium-low. Add carrots, apple, and maple syrup. Cover; simmer for 8 minutes or until desired doneness. Using slotted spoon, transfer chops, carrots, and apples to platter; bring syrup mixture to boiling. Boil gently, uncovered, 1 to 2 minutes or until thickened. Pour over chops. Makes 4 servings.

Meat: Millionaire's Meatloaf

Recipe from William Reynolds | Adapted from David Burke

Time: 1 hour 30 minutes

For the Meatloaf
1 1/2 tablespoons olive oil
2 medium onions finely chopped
6 cloves garlic minced
2 pounds lean ground beef
2 large eggs
1/2 cup milk
1 cup fresh bread crumbs
1/4 cup Dijon style mustard
1/4 cup barbecue sauce
1 tablespoon well drained horseradish
1/4 cup flat leaf parsley finely chopped

1 teaspoon each salt & pepper
1 teaspoon fresh thyme minced
2 -3 cups croutons
For the Chili Shrimp
1 1/2 teaspoons mild or hot chili powder
1 1/2 teaspoons cayenne pepper
1 1/2 teaspoons paprika
1 1/2 tablespoons Wondra flour
4 jumbo shrimp peeled and deveined
1 teaspoon chili oil
mashed potato for serving with meatloaf

For the meatloaf: Preheat oven to 375 degrees. Place a large skillet over medium heat, and add the olive oil, onions and garlic. Sauté until translucent and tender, 3 to 4 minutes. Remove from heat and set aside to cool. In a large mixing bowl, combine ground beef, eggs and milk. Mix well by hand, and add bread crumbs, mustard, barbecue sauce, horseradish, and cooked onions and garlic. Mix again, and add the parsley, salt, pepper and thyme. Mix well until thoroughly combined. Spread the croutons across a shallow 8-inch-square baking dish. Top with the meatloaf mix, patting the surface so it is level. Bake until the internal temperature reads 165 degrees on an instant-read thermometer and the top is nicely browned, about 1 hour. Toward the end of baking, prepare the chili shrimp.

For the chili shrimp: In a small mixing bowl, combine the chili powder, cayenne pepper, paprika and flour. Dredge the shrimp in the mixture until well coated. Place a small skillet over medium heat, and add the chili oil. When it is hot, add the shrimp and cook for 2 minutes a side.

To finish, cut the meatloaf into 4 slices. Place a slice on each of 4 plates, and top with a chili shrimp. If desired, serve with mashed potatoes.

Note: To make croutons, toss cubes of white bread with a bit of olive oil, salt and pepper, and roast on a baking sheet at 400 degrees, stirring once or twice, until lightly browned, about 15 minutes.

© 2013 Jody Cooke

Meat: Olde World Pork & Apple Kraut

Recipe by Gordon Perry

4 -6 thick pork chops
1 can large sauerkraut
1 can small applesauce chunky

fresh slices of lemon
ketchup
1/2 cup bread crumbs

Pre-heat oven to 350F
Sprinkle breadcrumbs on top surface of pork chops. Add ketchup and top with lemon slice. Mix chunky apple sauce with sauerkraut. Lightly spray oven dish with canola cooking spray. Add chops and surround with apple-kraut mixture. Bake until pork is completely cooked ~45 -60 mintues. Serve with boiled red potatoes, an additional helping of apple sauce and a lettuce and tomato side salad.

Meat: Pam's Zesty Chili

Preparation: 10 minutes, Cook Time: 30 minutes   Yield: 6 -8 servings
This chili recipe is one of my staples. This recipe makes enough for several dinners. Serve over rice with a dollop of sour cream on top.

1 pound ground beef
1/4 - 1/2 cup onion chopped
1-2 clove Dorot frozen crushed garlic cubes
1 (7-ounce) can kernal corn niblets
1 (6-ounce) can tomato paste
1 (15-ounce) can drained kidney beans
1 (4-ounce) can drained mushroom pieces & stems

1 (14 1/2-ounce) can Delmonte diced tomatoes with zesty jalapenos
1 (15 1/2-ounce) can drained Goya Frijoles Negros Beans
1 package Tempo or McCormick chili mix
2 tablespoons olive oil

Heat a Dutch oven over high heat, add olive oil. Add chopped onion when oil is hot. Brown onions before adding ground beef and crushed garlic. Brown the meat. Add all the remaining ingredients, stir well and bring to boil. Cover and turn heat down to simmer. Let Chili simmer for 30 minutes - 1 hour. While the chili is cooking, make the rice. I use a Sanyo rice maker, which makes perfect rice in 30 minutes regardless of how many cups of rice are being made. For this quantity of chili, make 3 cups of rice - and you'll have plenty of rice left over to freeze with the chili for later meals.

Meat: Pastitsio (Greek Lasagna)

Preparation: 45 minutes, Cook Time: 1 hr   Yield: 8 servings

Photo for recipe from Pamela Eden | Source: foodnetwork.com

3 tablespoons good olive oil
1 1/2 cups chopped yellow onions (1 large)
1 pound lean ground beef
1 pound lean ground lamb
1/2 cup dry red wine
1 tablespoon minced garlic (3 large cloves)
1 tablespoon ground cinnamon
1 teaspoon dried oregano
1 teaspoon fresh thyme leaves
pinch of cayenne pepper
1 can (28 ounces) crushed tomato in puree
kosher salt and freshly ground black pepper

1 1/2 cups whole milk
1 cup heavy cream
4 tablespoons (1/2 stick) unsalted butter
1/4 cup all-purpose flour
1/4 teaspoon freshly grated nutmeg
salt and freshly ground black pepper
1 1/2 cups freshly grated parmesan or
  kasseri cheese
2 extra-large eggs, beaten
2/3 cup greek-style yogurt, such as fage total
3/4 pound small shells

For the sauce, heat the olive oil over medium-high heat in a large pot. Add the onion and saute for 5 minutes. Add the beef and lamb, and saute over medium heat for 8 to 10 minutes, until it's no longer pink, crumbling it with the back of wooden spoon. Drain off any excess liquid, add the wine, and cook for 2 more minutes. Add the garlic, cinnamon, oregano, thyme, and cayenne, and continue cooking over medium heat for 5 minutes. Add the tomatoes, 2 teaspoons salt, and 1 teaspoon pepper and simmer, stirring occasionally, for 40 to 45 minutes. Set aside. Preheat the oven to 350 degrees F. For the bechamel, heat the milk and cream together in a small saucepan over medium-low heat until simmering. In a medium saucepan, melt the butter. Add the flour and cook over medium heat, whisking constantly for 2 minutes. Pour the warm milk and cream mixture into the butter and flour mixture, whisking constantly. Continue cooking, stirring occasionally, over medium heat for 5 to 7 minutes, until smooth and thick. Add the nutmeg, 1 teaspoon salt, and 1 teaspoon of pepper. Stir in 3/4 cup of Parmesan cheese, 1/2 cup of the tomato and meat sauce, and allow to cool for 10 minutes. Stir in the eggs and yogurt and set aside. Meanwhile, cook the pasta in a large pot of boiling water until al dente. Don't over-cook because the pasta will later be baked. Drain and set aside. Add the pasta to the meat and tomato sauce, and pour the mixture into a baking dish. Spread the bechamel evenly to cover the pasta and sprinkle with the remaining 3/4 cup Parmesan cheese. Bake for 1 hour, until golden brown and bubbly. Set aside for 10 minutes and serve hot.

Meat: Pizza Rustica (Easter Pie)
Recipe from Marie Gelsomino

Filling
3 pounds ricotta cheese
2 pounds shredded mozzarella cheese
9 eggs
1-1/2 cup Romano cheese
4 3/4" slices salami cut into cubes
3 packages sweet sausages fried & cubed
1 package hot sausage fried & cubed

1 pound box elbow Macaroni cooked
Dough
6 -7-1/2 cups flour
1 cup +2 TBS oil
15 tablespoons water
3/4 cup sugar
6 eggs

Cook sausages until browned. Peel off casing, cut sausage into pieces. Cut ham and salami into 3/4" cubes. Mix eggs and cheeses together for filling. Add more eggs if necessary. Boil macaroni in salted water until al dente. Drain. Add meats to cheese mixture. Fold in macaroni.

Prepare dough - mix dry ingredients together. Mix beaten eggs and oil together. Make a well in center of flour mixture and pour egg mixture. Knead ingredients together.
10. Add enough water to flour mixture to form a ball. Roll out enough dough to cover loaf pans or casserole dishes. Spoon in filling. Roll out dough for top crust. Moisten dough on bottom crust to attach top crust, crimp with fingers or a fork. Cut slits in top for steam to escape. Will a beaten egg, use a pastry brush to brush top crust. Sprinkle with sugar. Bake at 350F approx 2 hours or until crusts are well browned.

Notes: Prepare meats ahead of time. Cool sausages completely after cooking. For best results, use glass casserole dishes. If making multiple batches of dough, use less flour in proportion to the other ingredients. Start dough with the least amount of flour and add more flour as needed to achieve proper consistency.

Meat: Porchetta Pork Chops
Makes 2 servings
Recipe from William Reynolds

2 bone-in pork chops 1-1/2 inch thick
1 teaspoon coarse kosher salt
1 lemon
2 cloves garlic minced
2 tablespoons rosemary chopped

pinch red pepper flakes
1/2 teaspoon fennel seeds lightly crushed
2 tablespoons fennel fronds chopped
2 tablespoons olive oil

Heat oven to 350F. Pat pork chops dry and using a very sharp paring knife, cut a large pocket into the fat-covered edge of each chop. Season chops all over with 1 tsp salt, including inside pockets. Finely grate zest from lemon and put in a small bowl. Cut lemon lengthwise in quarters for serving.

Using a mortar and pestle or the flat side of a knife, mash garlic with a pinch of salt until you get a paste. Add to the bowl with the lemon zest and stir in rosemary, red pepper flakes, fennel seeds, 2 TB fennel fronds and 2 TB olive oil. Divide filling between pork chops, stuffing some inside pockets and rubbing the rest on the outside. Heat a large ovenproof skillet over high heat and add 1 TB olive oil. Sear pork chops on one side for 5 minutes, or until golden brown. Gently turn over chops and cook for another minute, then transfer skillet to oven. Cook until meat is just done, about 5 -10 minutes longer. Transfer pork chops to plate, tent with foil and let rest for 10 minutes before serving. Garnish with fennel fronds and lemon wedges.

Sunhee Chung

Sunhee Chung

Meat: Saucy Meatballs

Cook Time: 25 minutes
Recipe by Deette Little

2 pounds ground beef
1 cup bread crumbs

1 can cream of mushroom soup
1 can water

Note - an electric frying pan works great for this. Mix bread crumbs and ground beef until well blended. Shape into meatballs and brown in a frying pan which has been sprayed with nonstick cooking spray.   Mix mushroom soup and water together and add to meatballs. Simmer about 20 -25 minutes covered. Baste meatballs occasionally.

Serve over rice or noodles or as an appetizer alone.

Meat: Slow Cooker - Pork Roast with Peach Sauce   Makes 8 servings

Preparation: 10 minutes, Cook Time: 3 hours on High or 6 hours on Low
Recipe from Pamela Eden

1 (~3 pounds) boneless pork loin
1/4 teaspoon onion salt
1/4 teaspoon pepper
1 (15-ounce) can sliced peaches in heavy
  syrup
1/2 cup chili sauce

1/3 cup packed light brown sugar
3 tablespoons apples cider vinegar
1 teaspoon pumpkin pie spice
1 tablespoon cornstarch mixed with 2 TB
  Water
cooked egg noodles optional

Coat a 6 qt slow cooker with nonstick cooking spray. Place roast into slow cooker, season with onion salt and black pepper . Drain peaches, reserving the syrup. In a bowl, whisk syrup, chili sauce, brown sugar, vinegar and pumpkin pie spice. Pour over meat. Scatter peach slices over the roast. Cook 3 hours on High or 6 hours on Low. Remove meat and allow to rest for 10 minutes. Spook out peach slices and reserve. Place liquid in a small saucepan and bring to a boil over medium-high heat. Stir in cornstarch mixture and cook, stirring for about 30 seconds until sauce thickens.

To serve, slice meat and scatter reserved peach slices over the top. Serve with sauce on the side and egg noodles if desired.

Photography by Pamela (c) 1998

Meat: Slow-cooker Italian-Style Steak with Mushrooms & Onions

Makes 4 servings

Preparation: 15 minutes, Cook Time: 6 hr High / 8 hr Low
Recipe from Pamela Eden
Souce: Familycircle.com

1-1/2 pound boneless beef chuck Cut into 4 equal "steak" slices
1 teaspoon dried Italian seasoning
1/4 teaspoon salt
1/4 teaspoon pepper
2 cubanelle pepper seeds removed & sliced
1 red sweet pepper seeds removed & sliced
1 sweet onion sliced

1 (10-ounce) package white mushrooms quartered
1/2 cup beef broth
2 tablespoons red wine vinegar
1 tablespoon Worcestershire sauce
1 tablespoon brown sugar
fresh basil leaves
fresh tube polenta sliced into rounds and grilled

To make clean up easier - coat bowl of slow cooker with nonstick cooking spray or use a slow cooker liner. Season both sides of steaks with Italian seasoning, salt and pepper. Place in slow cooker. Scatter Cubanelle peppers, red pepper, onion and mushrooms over top. In a small bowl, combine broth, vinegar, Worcestershire sauce and brown sugar. Pour over peppers, mushrooms and onions. Cover and cook on High for 6 hours or Low for 8 hours. Serve steaks with pepper, mushrooms, onions and some of the cooking liquid spooned over the top. Garnish with basil and if desired serve with grilled polenta rounds.

Pasta: Cheeseburger Noodle Bake

Makes 6 servings

Cook Time: 25 minutes
Recipe by Deette Little

1 1/2 pounds ground beef
1 teaspoon Worcestershire sauce
4 lasagna noodles
White Sauce
2 tablespoons butter or margarine

1 small onion chopped
2 tablespoons all purpose flour
1 cup milk
8 slices yellow American cheese

Cook noodles according to package directions. Combine ground beef and Worcestershire sauce. Make 6 hamburger patties and brown both sides in a frying pan. In another pan, melt butter and add chopped onion and cook until translucent. Stir in all purpose flour. Add milk and continue to cook and stir until thickened. Place a layer of 2 noodles in a 9 x 12 baking pan. Top with half of the white sauce. Cut 5 slices of cheese into small pieces and sprinkle half of the cheese on the sauce. Repeat the layer of noodles, sauce and cheese. Top with the hamburger patties and bake at 350F for 20 minutes. Cut the remaining 3 slices of cheese into triangle halves and place one triangle on each burger. Return to the oven for 2 minutes until the cheese is melted.

Pasta: Funky Spaghetti

Cook Time: 8 -10 minutes

Yield: 3 -4 servings

Recipe and photo from Patti Tivnan (Source: Jamie Oliver via Oprah.com)

This is a delicious super quick light Summer supper that takes advantage of Summer's garden bounty.

1 pound multigrain Barilla Plus spaghetti or linguine
11-14 ounces cherry tomatoes red & yellow
handful fresh basil leaves - torn
fresh or dried marjoram

6-8 glugs extra virgin olive oil
1 clove garlic peeled and finely chopped
splash red wine vinegar
salt and pepper

Put pasta in large pot of boiling water and cook until al dente. Slit tomatoes and tear basil apart with your fingers. Put in a bowl and add herbs, olive oil, garlic and vinegar.
Use tongs to remove pasta from the cooking water, and while still steaming, mix with the tomatoes. Adjust seasoning to taste. Separate onto plates and serve.

Pasta: Spaghetti Pie

Makes 6 servings

Recipe from Kathleen Jusko

6 ounces spaghetti
2 tablespoons margarine
1/3 cup grated Parmesan cheese
2 eggs well beaten
1 pound ground beef and/or sausage
1/2 cup onion chopped
1 (8-ounce) can tomato diced

1 (6-ounce) can tomato paste
1 teaspoon sugar
1 teaspoon oregano
1/2 teaspoon garlic powder
1 cup cottage cheese (or ricotta cheese)
1/2 cup mozzarella cheese

Cook spaghetti, drain and stir in butter. Add Parmesan cheese and eggs. Form into crust in a buttered 10" pie plate. Brown beef, onions, peppers till tender. Drain off excess fat. Stir in Undrained tomatoes, tomato paste, sugar, oregano, garlic powder, salt. Heat through. Spread cottage cheese over bottom area crust. Fill pie with meat mixture. bake uncovered in 350F oven 20 minutes then sprinkle mozzarella over pie and bake until cheese melts 5 minutes.

Pasta: Stir-fried Soba Noodles with Long Beans, Eggs and Cherry Tomatoes

Recipe from William Reynolds

Tomatoes and noodles Asian style, the cherry tomatoes are cooked just to the point at which their skins split allowing the fruit inside to soften just a little and sweeten a lot.

- 8 ounces soba noodles
- salt to taste
- 2 teaspoons sesame oil
- 1/2 cup chicken or vegetable stock
- 2 tablespoons soy sauce
- 2 teaspoons rice vinegar
- 1/2 teaspoon sugar
- 2 tablespoons peanut, grapeseed or canola oil
- 2 large eggs beaten
- 1 -2 green jalapeno chiles minced
- 2 cloves garlic minced
- 1 tablespoon ginger minced
- 3/4 pound purple or green beans cut into 1" pieces
- 1 pound cherry tomato
- 1/4 teaspoon ground black pepper
- 1 cup cilantro chopped

First cook the Soba Noodles. bring 3 or 4 Qts of water to a boil in a large pot. Add salt to taste. Add the noodles gradually, so that the water remains at a boil. Stir once with a long handled spoon or pasta fork so the noodles don't stick together. Wait for the water to back to a rolling boil- it will bubble up. Add 1 cup of cold water. Allow the water to come back to a rolling boil, and add another cup of water. Repeat this one more time and add a 3rd cup of cold water. When the water boils again the noodles should be cooked through. Drain and toss with sesame oil in a bowl and set aside.

Mix together the stock, soy sauce, rice vinegar and sugar in a small bowl. Mix the minced chiles, garlic and ginger in another bowl. Place all the ingredients within reach of your wok.

Heat a 14 inch flat bottomed wok over high heat until a drop of water evaporates within a second when added to the pan. Beat 1 of the eggs in a bowl and add salt to taste. Swirl 1 tsp of the oil into the wok and add the egg, using a rubber spatula to scrape out every last bit. Tilt the wok to spread the egg into a pancake and cook until set ~ 30 sec to 1 minute. Using a metal spatula, flip over and cook for another 5 seconds, then transfer to a cutting board. Cut egg into 2 inch long by 1/4 inch wide slices. Repeat with the other egg.

Add the remaining oil to the wok, swirl the pan, then add the garlic,ginger and chile and stirfry for no more than 10 seconds. Add the long beans and stirfry for 1 minute. Add the tomatoes and stirfry for 2 minutes or until they collapse a little in the wok. Add the noodles, stock and salt. Turn the heat down to medium and fry for about 1 minute until the liquid has evaporated. Sprinkle with pepper, add the eggs and cilantro. Continue to fry until heated through and serve.

Advance Prep: The Soba Noodles can be cooked up to a day in advance. Refrigerate until added to the wok.

Pasta: Stuffed Shells

Recipe from Marie Gelsomino

1 jar small tomato sauce
1/2 box jumbo pasta shells
FILLING
2 pounds ricotta cheese
1 tablespoon chopped parsley

1/2 pound (1 cup) mozzarella cheese
shredded
2 large eggs
1/2 cup grated Romano cheese

Filling: Mix ricotta cheese and chopped parsley together. Add eggs and mozzarella cheese. Add Parmesan or romano cheese to mixture for flavor

Pasta: Boil pasta shells until al dente, drain. Put in pan and replace with cold water

Casserole: Make a bed of tomato sauce in a 13x9x2" casserole dish. Spoon filling into cooled shells. Pack tightly into casserole dish. Spoon tomato sauce between shells. Bake at 400F for 30-45 minutes or until golden brown crust forms on filling.

Poultry: Cashew Chicken with Noodles Recipe

Preparation: 10 minutes, Cook Time: 10 minutes   Yield: 4 Servings

Source: tasteofhome.com

8 ounces uncooked thick rice noodles
1/4 cup soy sauce
2 tablespoons cornstarch
3 garlic cloves, minced
1 pound boneless skinless chicken breast,
cubed

1 tablespoon peanut oil
1 tablespoon sesame oil
6 green onions, cut into 2-inch pieces
1 cup unsalted cashews
2 tablespoons sweet chili sauce

Cook rice noodles according to package directions. Meanwhile, in a small bowl, combine the soy sauce, cornstarch and garlic. Add chicken. In a large skillet, saute chicken mixture in peanut and sesame oils until no longer pink. Add onions; cook 1 minute longer. Drain noodles; stir into skillet. Add cashews and chili sauce and heat through. Yield: 4 servings.

Poultry: Chicken and Bok Choy Stir Fry

Recipe from William Reynolds

- 2 tablespoons soy sauce
- 2 tablespoons rice wine vinegar
- 1 1/2 tablespoons sesame oil
- 2 teaspoons light brown sugar
- 3/4 pound boneless chicken thigh cut into
    - 1/2" strips
- 2 tablespoons ginger root minced
- 2 cloves garlic chopped
- 3 tablespoons peanut oil or vegetable oil
- 1/2 pound bok choy (1 head) trimed & sliced
- 2 (1/2 pound) leeks halved & thinly sliced
- pinch red pepper flakes
- pinch salt
- cooked rice for serving

In a medium bowl, whisk together soy sauce, vinegar, sesame oil, and sugar. Pour half the mixture over the chicken, along with half the ginger and half the garlic. Let stand 30 minutes. Heat a large, 12-inch skillet over high heat until extremely hot, about 5 minutes. Add 1 tablespoon peanut oil and the chicken. Cook, stirring constantly, until meat is cooked through, about 3 minutes. Transfer to a plate. Add the remaining peanut oil to the skillet. Add the bok choy and cook 1 minute. Stir in the leeks and chili flakes; cook, tossing frequently until bok choy and leeks are tender, about 1 minute. Stir in the marinade and a pinch of salt. Move vegetable mixture to the border of the pan. Add remaining ginger and garlic to center of pan and cook, mashing lightly, until fragrant, about 30 seconds. Return chicken to skillet and combine with ginger, garlic, and vegetables. Serve immediately, over rice.

Poultry: Chicken with Pineapple (for 2)
Makes 2 servings

Recipe from Patti Tivnan.

This recipe may be made with or without the batter coating. Both ways are yummy!

- BATTER(optional)
- 1 cup flour
- 3/4 cup water
- 1/2 teaspoon salt
- 1 egg
- SAUCE
- 1 tablespoon soy sauce
- 2 tablespoons sugar
- 2 teaspoons red wine vinegar
- 1 tablespoon cooking white wine (or rice wine)
- 1/2 cup pineapple juice
- 2 teaspoons cornstarch
- 1/2 teaspoon ginger
- 1-2 chopped spring onions or sugar snap peas

Mix batter ingredients and set aside for 1 hour. Cut 1/2 - 1 lb chicken into bite sized pieces. If using the coating for chicken, heat oil in wok. Dip chicken in coating and fry until golden brown. Drain on paper towel. If not coating chicken, saute the chicken thoroughly in wok or frying pan in a bit of oil. Cut 1 -2 pineapple slices into bite sized pieces and add to the chicken, cooking both until lightly browned. Add about a cup of juice to moisten the chicken mixture.

In a bowl, combine the following to thicken sauce (quantities depending upon the number of portions, taste etc.) Add sauce to pineapple and chicken pieces and juice in the wok, stir until sauce thickens. Throw in the sugar snap peas or spring onions just before serving and cook less than a minute. Serve with rice.

Poultry: Chicken, Mushrooms, Goat Cheese Wraps

Preparation: 10 minutes, Cook Time: 5 minutes

**1 (12-ounce) package mixed mushrooms
   sliced
1 rotissery chicken
2 roasted red bell peppers (optional)
130 grams goat cheese**

**sprouts or lettuce
flour tortilla
1/4 cup pesto (or wasabi optional)
1/4 cup mayonnaise
1 teaspoon chile sauce or hot sauce**

Lightly oil a large frying pan over medium high heat. Add mushrooms - sprinkle with salt & pepper. Cook about 5 minutes until mushrooms are softened. Remove skin from chicken and shred meat or cut into bite-size pieces. Pat peppers dry and slice into strips. Spread wraps with mayo and dollops of pesto. Add layer of lettuce or sprouts
Arrange peppers, chicken and mushrooms and roll up wrap. Use toothpicks to hold closed. Slice in half.

Poultry: Crockpot Turkey Breast

Preparation: 10 minutes, Cook Time: 8 hours
Recipe from Carol Southerland

**2 - 3 1/2 pounds frozen turkey breast
1/2 cup orange juice
1/2 cup water**

**1 teaspoon dried rosemary
1/2 teaspoon dried thyme**

Place frozen turkey breast in crockpot. Pour orange juice and water over turkey. Sprinkle spices over top. Cover and cook on low 7 -8 hours.

Carol Southerland

Poultry: Indonesian Ginger Chicken

Preparation: 15 min, Cook Time: 1 hr 0 min   Yield: 4 to 6 servings

Recipe forwarded by Pamela Eden | Source: foodnetwork.com

1 cup honey
3/4 cup soy sauce
1/4 cup minced garlic (8 to 12 cloves)

1/2 cup peeled and grated fresh ginger root
(1- 4 oz jar of minced ginger)
2 (3 1/2 pound) chickens, quartered, with
backs removed

Cook the honey, soy sauce, garlic, and ginger root in a small saucepan over low heat until the honey is melted. Arrange the chicken in 1 layer in a 13 x 9 lasagna pan baking pan, skin side down, and pour on the sauce. Cover the pan tightly with aluminum foil. Marinate overnight in the refrigerator.

Preheat the oven to 350 degrees F. Place the covered baking pan in the oven and bake for 30 minutes. Uncover the pan, turn the chicken skin side up, and raise the temperature to 375 degrees F. Continue baking for 30 minutes or until the juices run clear when you cut between a leg and thigh and the sauce is a rich, dark brown.

Serve with Jasmine rice (2 cups rice made with 1 can coconut milk and 3 cups water)

Kathleen Jusko

Kathleen Jusko

Poultry: Persian Style Chicken with Walnut, Onion & Pomegranate Sauce

Makes 6 servings

Preparation: 10 minutes, Cook Time: 40 minutes
Recipe from Pamela Eden

3 tablespoons olive oil
2 1/2 - 3 pounds chicken
2 medium onions thinly sliced
1 teaspoon cinnamon
2 cups toasted walnuts or pecans, coarsly chopped
2/3 cup pomegranate juice

1/2 cup tomato sauce
1 1/2 cups no sodium, fat free chicken broth
1 tablespoon + 1 teaspoon lemon juice
1/4 teaspoon salt
1/4 teaspoon pepper
1 tablespoon molasses dark preferrably

Heat oil in a large Dutch oven. Saute chicken turning occasionally 10 -15 minutes until brown on all sides. Transfer chicken to plate. Reduce heat and add onion to juices in dutch oven and saute until golden & soft. Add cinnamon and stir for about 1 minute. Add walnuts and cook for about 1 minute. Add juice, broth, tomato sauce, molasses and spices. Bring to boil and then reduce to simmer for 3- 5 minutes. Add chicken pieces (without juice) to pot and simmer covered for 15 -20 minutes until chicken is cooked through.

Good served with Jasmine rice or noodles

Poultry: Saltimbocca Chicken

Preparation: 1 hour, Cook Time: 30 minutes
Recipe from William Reynolds

Yield: 4 - 6 servings

1 1/2 pounds boneless, skinless chicken breasts cut into 4 oz pieces
dash salt & pepper
1 tablespoon sage chopped, plus 24 large leaves

2 cloves garlic mashed to paste
pinch red pepper flakes optional
olive oil
6 slices thin prosciutto
6 slices fontina cheese (about 4 oz)

Using a meat mallet, pound the chicken to flatten a bit. Salt and pepper each piece on both sides and place on a platter. Sprinkle with chopped sage, garlic, red pepper flakes (if using) and olive oil. Massage in the seasoning to distribute, cover and marinate for at least an hour at room temperature (or refrigerate overnight). Heat a wide skillet over medium heat and add 3 tablespoons olive oil. When the oil looks wavy, add the sage leaves and let them crisp for about 30 seconds. Remove and drain. Brown the chicken breasts in the oil for about 2 minutes per side, then transfer to a baking dish large enough to fit them in one layer. Top each piece with 2 sage leaves, a slice of prosciutto and a slice of fontina. Broil for 2 to 3 minutes, until the cheese is bubbling. Garnish with remaining sage leaves.

Poultry: Sesame Chicken

Cook Time: 1 hr 20 minutes
Recipe from Merle Morse

1 1/2 - 2 cups sweet and sour sauce
1 large onion sliced
1 teaspoon garlic powder
1/4 cup sesame seeds

1 (14-ounce) can pineapple chunks
1/4 - 1/2 cup slivered almonds
1 (11-ounce) can mandarin orange segments
8 -10 pieces chick legs & thighs

Pre-heat oven to 350F.   Spread onion across bottom of 9 x13 baking pan. Cover with sweet n sour sauce. Arrange chicken on top of sauce. Pour juice from pineapple chunks over chicken. Arrange pineapple and mandarin orange segments over chicken. Sprinkle with sesame seeds and almonds. Place covered pan on cookie sheet in oven and bake 1 hour. Remove from oven and remove cover. Add more fruit and sesame seeds if desired and return to oven for another 15 -20 minutes until tops are browned.

Poultry: Thai Red Chicken Curry

Preparation: 10 minutes, Cook Time: 15 minutes   Yield: 4 Servings

Recipe from Pamela Eden | Source: tasteofhome.com

1 can coconut milk
1/3 cup chicken broth
2 tablespoons brown sugar
2 tablespoons fish sauce (soy sauce could be substituted)

1 tablespoon red curry paste
2 cups frozen stir-fry vegetables blend
3 cups cubed cooked chicken breasts
cooked jasmine rice
minced fresh cilantro, optional

Combine the first five ingredients in a large skillet. Bring to a boil; reduce heat and simmer 5 minutes. Stir in vegetables; return to a boil. Reduce heat and simmer, uncovered, for 9-11 minutes or until vegetables are tender and sauce thickens slightly.   Add chicken; heat through. Serve with rice. Sprinkle with cilantro if desired.

Quiche - Golden Corn Quiche

Cook Time: 45 minutes
Recipe from Marie Gelsomino

Crust
1-1/2 cup flour
1/2 teaspoon salt
1/2 cup butter flavored shortening
4-5 tablespoons cold water
Filling
1-1/3 cup half and half

3 eggs
3 tablespoons butter melted
1/2 small onion cut into wedges
1 tablespoon all purpose flour
1 tablespoon sugar
1 teaspoon salt
2 cups frozen corn thawed

Crust: Mix Flour and salt together. Cut in shortening with pastry cutter. Blend until crumbs are the size of small peas. Gradually add water until a ball forms. Roll dough between 2 sheets of wax paper. Remove 1 sheet of wax paper and drape pastry into pie plate. Remove second sheet of wax paper.

Filling: Line unpricked pastry shell with a double thickness of heavy duty aluminum foil. Bake at 375F for 5 minutes. In a blender combine the cream, eggs, butter, onion, flour, salt and sugar. Cover well and process until well blended. Stir in corn and pour into crust. Bake for 35 -40 minutes until a knife in center comes out clean. Let stand for 30 minutes before cutting.

Quiche: Onion Pie

Cook Time: 45 minutes
Recipe from Marie Gelsomino

Yield: 6 -8 servings

5 cups (5 medium) onions thinly sliced
2 tablespoons vegetable oil
1/2 teaspoon salt

1 egg
1 cup half and half
1 pastry crust

Prepare Pie crust dough. Roll out crust, place crust in a 9" round casserole dish. Press onto bottom and sides of dish. In a large skillet, saute onion in vegetable oil until tender, sprinkle with salt. Spoon onions into crust. In a bowl, beat egg and half-half. Pour milk mixture over onions. Bake, uncovered at 375F for 15 minutes. Reduce heat to 325F for 25-30 minutes longer or until knife inserted in center comes out clean.

Carol Zielinski

Quiche: Tom Gibson's Very Good Swiss Quiche (Cheese & Onion Pie)

Cook Time: 30 minutes

Recipe from Pamela Eden

I met Tom when I was attending the University of Alberta in Edmonton, Alberta, Canada. He had his own house (which was unique among us grad students and he had a sense of "self" that was different from anyone else I knew. On Sunday afternoons, he'd invite us over to make croissants or pasta from scratch, then we'd get to eat using his completely mismatched china & silverware. It was fascinating for someone like me who grew up in a home where everything matched.

3 -4 thinly sliced onions
2 tablespoons olive oil
2 eggs
2 egg yolk
1 cup milk
1/2 cup cream or evaporated milk

3/4 teaspoon salt
1/2 teaspoon pepper
1/8 teaspoon nutmeg
1/2 cup gruyére cheese
1/2 cup sharp cheddar cheese

Heat oven to 450F. Heat 2 TB Oil in heavy skillet. Add onions and toss to coat with the oil. Cover tightly and steam over low heat until tender but not brown. Remove lid for last minute to evaporate accumulated moisture. Beat in a small bowl: eggs, egg yolks, milk, cream, spices, and cheese. Arrange onions evenly in a 9 inch unbaked pieshell

Pour milk-egg-cheese mixture over the onions. Bake 10 minutes at 450, then reduce heat to 350 and bake 20 minutes or until Quiche is set and puffy. Enjoy with friends.

Quick Prep Kielbasa, Kraut & Potato Skillet Dinner

Recipe by Gordon Perry

kielbasa cut into 1/2 - 3/4" slices
green or red cabbage cut into 1" slices

potato cut into 1" slices
salt & pepper

Heat frying pan on medium heat with small amount of canola oil. Add all ingredients. Cover pan and let cook until potatoes and cabbage are soft. Serve with chunky apple sauce and side salad.

Savory: Fresh Mushroom Pie

Recipe from Pamela Eden

This is great with a side salad, slices of fresh Jersey tomato, a little wedge of cheese and some Branson pickle. Perfect for lunch with friends.

8 ounces fresh mushrooms cleaned
1 tablespoon unsalted butter
2 teaspoons all purpose flour
1 cup all purpose flour
1-1/2 teaspoon baking powder
1/2 teaspoon salt

1 small onion
1/4 cup olive oil
1/4 cup milk or chicken broth
dash pepper or Mrs Dash
1 egg white beaten slightly

To make filling, finely chop mushrooms and onion. Melt butter in a large skillet over medium heat. Add mushrooms and onion. Cook about 5 -7 minutes, stirring often until any liquid has evaporated. Remove from heat. Stir in 2 Tablespoons of flour, pepper and seasonings. Spread filling on a plate to cool quickly. Heat oven to 425F.

To make crust, mix 1 cup flour, baking powder and salt in a large bowl. Add olive oil and milk or chicken broth. stir to make a smooth pastry dough. Cut dough in half. On an ungreased cookie sheet without sides, roll out one half of the dough between 2 sheets of waxed paper into an 9 inch circle. Spread mushroom filling over dough on the cookie sheet to within 1 inch of the edge. Peel wax paper off the other circle of dough. Lift the bottom sheet and flip dough over on top of the filling. Peel off the wax paper, fold over the edges of the dough and pat or crimp lightly. Cur four 2 inch slits in the top crust so steam can escape. Brush top crust with egg white.

Bake 18 -20 minutes or until pale brown. Slide pie onto wire rack to cool about 10 minutes. Serve with tomato wedges. cheese, green salad with light vinegar dressing.

Patti Tivnan

Seafood: Fillet of Cod with Asparagus & Prosciutto

Makes 6 servings

Cook Time: 12 minutes
Recipe from Willam Reynolds | Source Bon Appetit 04/2004.

Each serving is baked en papillote (wrapped in parchment paper) to lock in steam for succulent results.

- 1-1/2 pound slender asparagus spears 7" lengths
- 2 cloves garlic minced
- 1 teaspoon salt
- 2 tablespoons butter
- 1 tablespoon +6 tsp olive oil
- 1/3 cup fresh lemon juice
- 1-1/2 teaspoon lemon peel grated
- 1/2 teaspoon pepper
- 6 (6-ounce) slices cod filets pinbones removed
- 6 ounces prosciutto slices halved

Cook asparagus in large pot of boiling salted water until crisp- tender, about 3 minutes. Drain. Transfer to bowl of ice water to cool. Drain well. Mash garlic and 1 tsp salt to paste in small bowl. Melt butter with 1 TB oil in small nonstick skillet over medium heat. Add garlic paste, stir until pale golden about 1 minute. Stir in lemon juice, peel and 1/2 tsp black pepper. Remove from heat.

Pre-heat oven to 500F. Cut out six 12-inch squares of parchment paper. Place 1 parchment square on work surface. Drizzle 1 tsp oil over parchment. Place 1 cod fillet in center of parchment. Spoon 1/6 of garlic-lemon mixture over fish. Cover 1/6 of asparagus spears. Arrange 1/6 of prosciutto slices over. Fold 2 opposite sides of parchment in over fish and vegetables, then fold in remaining 2 sides, enclosing completely. Fasten parchment edges together with paper clips to seal packet. Place on large rimmed baking sheets. Repeat procedure with remaining parchment, oil,fish, garlic-lemon mixture, asparagus and prosciutto (Can be prepared 6 hours ahead and refrigerated). Bake fish until just opaque in center (Parchment will turn golden brown) about 12 minutes. Transfer 1 parchment packet to each plate to serve.

Jusko

Seafood: Lime Broiled Catfish Recipe

Preparation: 10 minutes, Cook Time: 5 minutes

Recipe from Marie Gelsomino | Source: tasteofhome.com

1 tablespoon butter
2 tablespoons lime juice
1/2 teaspoon salt, optional
1/4 teaspoon pepper

1/4 teaspoon garlic powder
2 catfish fillets (6 ounces each)
slice lime or wedges, optional
fresh parsley, optional

Melt butter in a small saucepan. Stir in the lime juice, salt if desired, pepper and garlic powder. Remove from the heat and set aside. Place fillets in a shallow baking pan. Brush each fillet generously with lime-butter sauce. Broil for 5-8 minutes or until fish flakes easily with a fork. Remove to a warm serving dish; spoon pan juices over each fillet. Garnish with lime slices and parsley if desired. Yield: 2 servings.

Seafood: Maple- Soy Salmon

Cook Time: 20 minutes
Recipe from Pamela Eden

1/4 cup maple syrup
2 tablespoons soy sauce
1 clove garlic minced

1/4 teaspoon garlic salt
1/8 teaspoon pepper
1 pound salmon

In a small bowl mix maple syrup, soy, garlic and pepper. Place Salmon in shallow glass dish and coat with maple mix. Cover dish and marinate in refrigerator for 30 minutes, turning 1 time. Pre-heat oven to 400F. Place baking dish in oven and bake uncovered for 20 minutes or until fish easily flakes.

May be served hot over rice or cold over mixed salad greens.

Seafood: Roasted Salmon with Herb Vinaigrette   Makes 2 servings

Cook Time: 40 minutes
Recipe from William Reynolds

olive oil
1 1/2 medium Idaho potatoes peeled & cut
   into slices
kosher salt & pepper
1/4 cup red wine vinegar
1 teaspoon Dijon style mustard
1 clove garlic minced

1/2 teaspoon fresh rosemary finely chopped
1/2 teaspoon fresh sage finely chopped
1/2 teaspoon fresh thyme finely chopped
1 tablespoon fresh parsley finely chopped
6 tablespoons olive oil
2 Filets 4 - 6 oz each salmon skinned

Heat oven to 400 degrees. Brush two 8-inch terra-cotta cazuelas or other shallow baking dishes with olive oil. Arrange potato slices in a single layer in bottom of each. Brush potatoes with olive oil, and season with salt and pepper. Bake 12 to 15 minutes. While potatoes bake, whisk together vinegar, mustard, garlic and herbs in a medium-size bowl. Slowly whisk in 6 tablespoons olive oil, until emulsified. Season with salt and pepper to taste, and set aside. Brush salmon fillets with olive oil, and season with salt and pepper. When potatoes are done, remove cazuelas and reduce oven temperature to 250 degrees. Place fillets on top of potatoes, skinned side down. Roast 12 minutes. Remove salmon from oven, and drizzle each fillet with vinaigrette. Serve.

Seafood: Speedy Spicy Cod   Makes 4 servings

Cook Time: 30 minutes
Recipe by Pamela Eden

1 cup pearl barley
1 medium sweet potato peeled and chopped
1 large red bell pepper
1 bunch green onion
1 (3-inch) piece peeled fresh ginger

1 tablespoon curry powder
2 (14 1/2-ounce) cans zesty diced tomatoes
   drained
4 (4-ounce) slices skinless cod filets

In a large microwave bowl,combine the barley and 3 cups of water. Cover with vented plastic wrap and microwave on high 10 minutes. Stir in Sweet potato. Cover with vented plastic wrap and microwave on high 15 minutes or until tender. Chop pepper, slice green onions, and grate ginger. Reserve 2 tablespoons of green onion for garnish. In a bowl, combine remaining green onions, red pepper, ginger and 1/4 teaspoon salt and black pepper. Coat a 12" skillet with non-stick cooking spray and heat on medium high. Add pepper mixture and cook 3 minutes or until lightly browned. Stirring often. Add curry powder, cook 1 minute stirring constantly. Stir in tomatoes, heat to boiling. Nestle cod filets into tomato mixture, cover and cook 5 -8 minutes or until cod turns opaque throughout. Serve cod mixture over barley and sweet potato. Garnish with green onions.

Pamela Eden

Seafood: Thai Style Tilapia Filets

Recipe from Pamela Eden

4 Filets Tilapia
1/2 cup coconut milk (1/2 can)
3 tablespoons sliced almonds
2 tablespoons white onions chopped
1/2 teaspoon ground turmeric
1 teaspoon dried or fresh lemon grass chopped

1/4 teaspoon salt
1/2 teaspoon dried red pepper flakes
RICE
1/2 can coconut milk
2 cups jasmine rice
3 1/2 cups water
1 tablespoon olive oil

In medium size sauce pan, combine water, Coconut milk, oil and Jasmine rice. Bring to boil, stir, cover and reduce to simmer for 25 - 30 minutes.

Prepare fish while rice is cooking: Using a blender - combine Coconut milk, almonds, onion, tumeric, lemon grass & salt. Process until smooth. Heat a large nonstick skillet over med-high heat. Season filets with salt & pepper on both sides and place in skillet. Pour pureed sauce over filets, covering filets and sprinkle with red pepper flakes. Reduce heat to medium and simmer 15 minutes until puree is thickened and fish flakes easily.

Gordon Perry

Chapter 7: Vegetables

Patti Tivnan

Candied Ginger Carrots

Recipe from Maureen Heritage

3/4 cup firmly packed brown sugar
1/2 cup orange juice
2 tablespoons butter or margarine
1/2 teaspoon salt

1/4 teaspoon ground ginger
2 pounds medium sized carrots cut into 1/8"
thick slices

Combine brown sugar, orange juice, butter, salt & ginger in a large frying pan; heat slowly, stirring constantly to boiling. Stir in carrots and cover. Simmer 25 minutes. Uncover, continue cooking, stirring several times 10 minutes longer or until carrots are tender and richly glazed. Spoon into a heated serving bowl, garnish with parsley.

Crab-Stuffed Potatoes

Cook Time: 20 minutes
Recipe from Marie Gelsomino

4 medium baked potatoes
1/2 cup margarine
1/2 cup light cream
4 tablespoons grated onions

1 cup sharp cheddar cheese grated
8 ounces crabmeat
dash paprika

Bake potatoes until done. Cut lengthwise in half. Scoop out potato. Whip potato with onion, cream, cheese and margarine. Fold in Crabmeat. Fill potato shells with potato-crabmeat mix and sprinkle with paprika. Bake at 325F for 20 minutes.

Eggplant Parmagiana

Cook Time: 40 minutes
Recipe from Marie Gelsomino

2 medium eggplant sliced 1/4" thick
1 jar tomato sauce
1-1/2 pound ground beef or sausage

12 ounces mozzarella cheese grated
raisins (optional)

Fry ground beef or sausage until juices run clear, drain. Pour tomato sauce in pan. Add raisins if desired. Slice eggplants approx 1/4" thick. Dredge eggplant slices in flour.
Make a bed of tomato sauce mixture in casserole dish. and layer eggplant and cheese on top of the tomato. Pour sauce over cheese. Make a second layer of eggplant and tomato sauce mixture. Top with cheese. Bake at 375F for approx 40 minutes or until sauce bubbles in center.

Roasted Brussel Sprouts

Cook Time: 40 minutes
Recipe from Pamela Eden

1-1/2 pound brussels sprouts
3 tablespoons olive oil

3/4 teaspoon kosher salt
1/2 teaspoon ground pepper

Pre-heat oven to 400F. Cut off stem ends and pull off any yellow outer leaves. Slice sprouts in half. Mix in bowl with olive oil, salt & pepper. Pour sprouts onto sheet pan and roast for 35 -40 minutes. Watch carefully to be sure they don't burn.

Roasted Carrots and Parsnips

Recipe from Pamela Eden

1 pound baby carrots
1 pound parsnip
3 tablespoons olive oil

2 tablespoons honey
coarse salt and pepper

Pre-heat oven to 400F. Peel carrots and parsnips and cut in half length-wise. Mix in bowl with olive oil, hone & spices till coated well. 10 minutes in oven then flip carrots and parsnips over and cook for another 10 minutes until soft and slightly carmelized.

Sweet and Sour Orange Beets
Makes 8 servings

Recipe from Maureen Heritage

3 tablespoons cornstarch
1/4 teaspoon salt
4 tablespoons butter melted

2 (1-pound) cans beets
3 tablespoons vinegar
2 tablespoons orange marmalade

Blend cornstarch and salt into melted butter. Add 1/2 cup liquid drained from beets. Cook until thickened, stirring. Add vinegar & orange marmalade. Heat until blended. Add drained beets. Simmer gently for 5 -10 minutes.

Triple-Onion Baked Potatoes

Recipe from Marie Gelsomino

4 large baking potatoes
1/2 cup finely chopped red onion
1/2 cup finely chopped yellow onion
1/2 cup sour cream

2 tablespoons milk
1 cup diced white American cheese
1/2 cup shredded Cheddar cheese
4 green onions finely sliced

Bake potatoes until done. While potatoes are baking, saute red and yellow onions until tender- set aside. When potatoes are cool enough to handle, cut in half lengthwise. Scoop out potato, leaving an 1/8" shell. In a mixing bowl beat the potato, milk and sour cream until creamy. Stir in sauteed onions and American cheese. Spoon into potato shells. Place filled potatoes on baking sheet. Bake at 400F for 25 minutes. Sprinkle with Cheddar Cheese. Bake 5 -10 minutes longer or until Cheddar Cheese is melted.

Chapter 8: Desserts & Sweets

Photo by Kathy Rupff

Chapter 8: Desserts & Sweets (Contents)

Kathy Rupff

Apple Bread Pudding with Caramel Sauce Recipe

Preparation: 50 minutes, Cook Time: 40 minutes

Source: tasteofhome.com

3/4 cup butter, cubed
4 cups chopped peeled tart apples (about 4 medium)
2 cups sugar
1/2 cup raisins
1/2 cup chopped walnuts
3 teaspoons ground cinnamon
2 teaspoons vanilla extract
Bread Pudding
6 eggs
2-1/2 cups 2% milk

1-1/2 cup plus 2 tablespoons sugar, divided
1 cup heavy whipping cream
1-1/2 teaspoon vanilla extract
dash ground nutmeg
1 loaf (1 pound) french bread, cut into 1-inch cubes
caramel sauce:
1 cup sugar
1/4 cup water
1 cup heavy whipping cream
2 tablespoons butter

Preheat oven to 350°. In a large skillet, heat butter over medium heat. Add apples, sugar, raisins, walnuts and cinnamon; bring just to a boil, stirring constantly. Reduce heat; simmer, uncovered, until apples are tender, stirring occasionally. Remove from heat; stir in vanilla. For bread pudding, in a large bowl, whisk eggs, milk, 1-1/2 cups sugar, cream, vanilla and nutmeg until blended. Stir in bread cubes and apple mixture. Transfer to a greased 13x9-in. baking dish. Sprinkle with remaining sugar. Bake, uncovered, 40-45 minutes or until a knife inserted near the center comes out clean. For caramel sauce, in a small heavy saucepan, combine sugar and water; stir gently to moisten all the sugar. Cook over medium-low heat, gently swirling pan occasionally, until sugar is dissolved. Cover; bring to a boil over medium-high heat. Cook 1 minute. Uncover pan; continue to boil until syrup turns a medium amber color. Immediately remove from heat and carefully stir in cream and butter. Serve with warm bread pudding. Yield: 16 servings (1-3/4 cups sauce).

Bread: Charles Ballard's Banana Bread

From Connie Spangler via Kathy Rupff

1 3/4 cups flour
1 cup sugar
1/2 cup brown sugar
1 teaspoon baking soda
1/2 teaspoon salt
1/2 teaspoon cinnamon
2 eggs

3 mashed ripe bananas
1/2 cup canola vegetable oil
1/4 cup plus 1 Tablespoon buttermilk or
 plain yogurt
1 teaspoon vanilla extract
1/2 cup milk chocolate chips
1/2 cup peanut butter chips

In a large bowl, stir together flour, sugars, baking soda, salt and cinnamon. In another bowl, combine eggs, bananas, oil, buttermilk and vanilla. Add to flour mixture, stirring just until moistened. Fold in chips. Pour into a greased 9 x 13" loaf pan. Bake at 325 for 1 hour 20 minutes or until toothpick inserted in center comes out clean. Cool on a rack 10 minutes before removing from the pan.

Tips for banana bread - DONT overmix the batter - just mix until it's just moistened- otherwise it will be tough. Banana bread best if it is wrapped up after it's cooled and served the following day.

Bread: Eggnog Quick Bread

Preparation: 25 minutes, Cook Time: 50 minutes   Yield: 1 large loaf
Recipe from Pamela Eden

2 1/4 cups all purpose flour
2 teaspoons baking powder
1/2 teaspoon salt
1/4 teaspoon freshly grated nutmeg
2 large eggs
1 cup sugar
1 cup dairy or canned eggnog
1/2 cup butter melted

1 teaspoon vanilla extract
1/2 teaspoon rum extract (optional)
1 cup toasted, slivered almonds
Eggnog Icing
2 tablespoons dairy or canned eggnog
 (enough to create thick icing)
2 cups powdered sugar

Pre-heat oven to 350F. Grease bottom and 1/2" up sides of a 9x5x3 inch loaf pan. Set aside. In a large bowl, combine flour, baking powder, salt and nutmeg. Make a well in the center of the flour mix and set aside. In a small bowl, beat eggs with a fork, stir in sugar, eggnog, melted butter, vanilla and if desired rum extract. Add egg mixture to the flour. Stir until just moistened (batter should be lumpy). Fold in toasted almonds (and any dried or candied fruit if desired). Spoon batter into prepared pan. Bake 9x5x3 inch pan for 50 -55 minutes until toothpick inserted in center comes out clean. Cool pan on wire rack for 10 minutes. Remove from pan and cool completely on rack. Wrap and store overnight. Make icing by adding eggnog by the tablespoon to powdered sugar and mixing until a thick icing forms. Drizzle loaf with icing and let icing set before serving.

Merle Morse

Merle Morse

Bread: Grandma Jones Bran Muffins

Cook Time: 20 minutes
Recipe from Pamela Eden -

1 tablespoon shortening
1 cup firmly packed brown sugar
1 egg
1/2 teaspoon nutmeg
1/2 teaspoon salt
1 teaspoon vanilla extract

1 teaspoon baking soda
1 cup buttermilk
1 cup dates chopped
2 cups bran
1 cup sifted flour
1/2 cup golden raisins (optional)

Mix shortening, sugar and egg. Add nutmeg, salt and vanilla. Mix baking soda with buttermilk and add to the shortening mix. Mix dates, bran and flour alternately to the wet mixture until all combined. Fold in raisins. Fill muffin cups 3/4 full and bake for 10 minutes at 350F and then reduce temperature to 325F for 10 minutes.

Bread: Jean's Chocolate Chip Pumpkin Bread

Cook Time: 45 minutes
Recipe from Jeanmarie Rose Perry

2 1/4 cups flour
2 teaspoons baking powder
1/2 teaspoon baking soda
2 teaspoons cinnamon
1 teaspoon nutmeg
1 cup canned pumpkin

1 cup sugar
1/2 cup milk
2 eggs
1/4 cup butter melted
1/4 cup semisweet chocolate chips

Pre-heat oven to 350F. Grease a loaf pan. Mix flour, baking powder, soda, cinnamon, nutmeg and sugar in a large bowl. Add pumpkin, milk, eggs and butter and mix on low speed. Stir in chips. Pour into well greased loaf pan. Bake for approx 45 minutes or until toothpick comes out clean. Makes 1 loaf or 3 small sized loaves. Allow loaf to cool before removing from pan. Good with butter or plain.

Bread: Plain Scones

Cook Time: 10 minutes
Recipe from Pamela Eden

I recorded this recipe while watching my Aunt Connie Lay in England. She also told me that sweeter fruit scones could be made by adding 5 Tablespoons caster sugar & 1/3 cup dried fruit to the bowl with the dry ingredients.

8 ounces flour
pinch salt
1 teaspoon baking soda

1 1/2 teaspoons cream of tartar
2 tablespoons butter
milk

Sift flour, salt. baking soda and cream of tartar in a bowl. Mix in enough milk to make soft but not sticky dough. Turn dough onto a floured surface and knead lightly. Then roll dough out to a thickness of 3/4" and cut into scones with 2 1/2" round or square cookie cutter. Bake at 425F for 10 minutes or until well risen and golden brown.

Caroline Goldsmith

Bread: Sticky Buns

Recipe from Kathleen Jusko.

See recipe for refrigerator dough in the Odds N Ends chapter.

**1 recipe Refrigerator bread dough (enough
   for 2 - 9x13 pans)
cinnamon
brown sugar
melted butter**

**Icing
2 cups powdered sugar
water added by Tablespoons until
   spreadable consistency**

Let dough rest on floured cloth for 10 minutes. Roll dough into 9 x12" rectangle. Brush with melted butter, then sprinkle with cinnamon to thoroughly cover surface. Then cover with a good layer of brown sugar. Starting at the wide edge, roll the (Jelly roll fashion) the dough and pinch the seam together. Cut 1-1/2" thick slices and place them cut side down in parchment lined 9 x13" pan. Place in warmed oven that has been heated for 2 minutes, then shut off. Let buns raise for 50 minutes or until doubled in size. Turn oven on to 400F and bake for 25 minutes. Let buns cool for a bit and then drizzle with icing.

Brownies: Decadent Chocolate Chip Cream Cheese Brownies

Recipe and photo by Kathie Rupff.

1 box brownie mix Make as instructed on box for cake style
Filling
1 (8-ounce) package cream cheese at room temp

1 egg
1/3 cup granulated sugar
1 (12-ounce) package sweet or semi-sweet chocolate chips

Follow directions for brownie mix - cake style. Mix room temp cream cheese, sugar and egg in small bowl until smooth and creamy. Add chocolate chips. Set aside. Pour prepared brownie batter into greased 9 x 13 glass pan. Plop large spoonfuls of cream cheese mixture on top of brownie batter into 12 sections (because you are making 12 large brownies). Of course, you may position the cream cheese part however you want! Bake at 350 for 45 minutes, or until toothpick comes out clean. Let cool and refrigerate. Serve with a dollop of Cool whip :)

Butterscotch Bliss Dessert

Preparation: 20 minutes, Cook Time: 4 hours
Recipe by Kathleen Jusko

1 1/2 cups graham cracker crumbs
sugar substitute = 1/2 cup sugar
6 tablespoons melted butter
2 (8-ounce) packages reduced fat cream
   cheese
3 cups cold fat-free milk divided

2 (1-ounce) packages sugar free instant
   butterscotch pudding
1 (8-ounce) carton frozen reduced fat
   whipped topping thawed
1/2 teaspoon rum extract

In a small bowl, combine the cracker crumbs, 1/4 cup sugar substitute and butter. Press into a 13 x 9 inch pan coated with cooking spray. In a small bowl, beat the cream cheese, 1/4 cup milk and remaining sugar substitute until smooth. Spread over crust. In another bowl, whisk remaining milk, pudding mix for 2 minutes. Let stand or till soft set. Gently spread over cream cheese layer. Combine whipped topping and extract. Spread over the top of the dessert. Refrigerate for at least 4 hours.

Cake - Margie's Kumquat Cake

Recipe from Pamela Eden. Source: www.kumquatgrowers.com
The Kumquat is a sweet/sour fruit and is a member of the citrus family. With a thick sweet peel and tart pulp, it is eaten skin and all (except the seeds). The majority of Kumquats are grown in St Joseph, Florida and are available from November to March.

I make this cake for my husband's birthday every year and it's so refreshing to taste the bright and fresh "orange" citrus flavor during the winter.

1 box yellow (lemon) cake mix
1 package instant lemon pudding mix
3/4 cup oil
1/2 cup kumquat puree
1/4 cup milk
4 eggs

1 teaspoon lemon juice
Glaze
1 cup confectioners' sugar
2 tablespoons margarine melted
1 teaspoon lemon juice
1/4 cup kumquat puree

Combine first 5 ingredients in bowl and beat well. Add eggs one at a time beating each well. Add lemon juice. Pour batter into a greased and floured bundt pan and bake at 325F for 45 -50 minutes. Remove from pan and pour on glaze.

Glaze: combine glaze ingredients and pour over cake. Use slices of kumquat to decorate the cake.

Puree Preparation: Wash fruit, cut in half (across not lengthwise) and remove seeds. Place fruit (peel & pulp) in a blender or food chopper (blender makes a finer puree). Do not cook. Use puree in recipe immediately or freeze in ziplock bags or other container. Puree can be stored for 6 months to a year. When using frozen puree, defrost and drain the excess liquid before using.

Kathy Rupff

K Rupff

Cake: **Cherry Crunch Dessert**

Cook Time: 45 minutes

1-1/2 cup flour
3/4 cup quick cooking rolled oats
1/2 - 3/4 cup firmly packed brown sugar
1/2 teaspoon baking soda

1/2 teaspoon salt
1/2 cup (1 stick) butter
1 (1-pound 5-ounce) can cherry pie filling

Preheat oven to 350F. In a large bowl, combine dry ingredients and mix well. Cut in softened butter and blend until particles are small and uniform. Pat half of crumb mixture in ungreased 9" square baking pan. Cover crumb layer evenly with pie filling. Sprinkle remaining crumb mixture over filling. Bake at 350F for 45 -50 minutes. Serve warm or cooled.

Cake: **Chocolate Chip Fudge Cake**

Cook Time: 60 minutes
Recipe from Marie Gelsomino

1 package devil's food cake mix
4 eggs
1 (3 1/2-ounce) package chocolate instant pudding & pie filling mix

1/4 cup oil
1 cup water
9 ounces milk chocolate chips
chocolate frosting mix

Preheat oven to 350F. Mix all ingredients except chocolate chips in a large bowl. Fold in chocolate chips. Pour mixture into a tube pan. Bake for approx 1 hour or until skewer inserted in center comes out clean. Cool pan on rack for 15-20 minutes. Invert cake onto a large plate. Cool completely before frosting.

Cake: **Chocolate Zucchini Cake**
Makes 24 servings

Preparation: 15 minutes, Cook Time: 50 minutes
Recipe from Pamela Eden. Adapted from Allrecipes.com

2 cups all purpose flour
2 cups white sugar
3/4 cup unsweetened cocoa powder
2 teaspoons baking soda
1 teaspoon baking powder
1/2 teaspoon salt

1 teaspoon cinnamon
4 large eggs
1 1/2 cups vegetable oil
3 cups grated zucchini
3/4 cup walnuts chopped- optional

Pre-heat oven to 350F. Grease and flour a 9 x 13 inch baking pan. In a medium bowl, stir together the flour, sugar, cocoa, baking soda, baking powder, salt & cinnamon. Add eggs and oil, mix well. Fold in the nuts and zucchini until they are evenly distributed. Pour into the prepared pan. Bake for 50 -60 minutes until a knife inserted in the center comes out clean. Cool the cake completely before frosting with either chocolate frosting, cream cheese frosting or easiest of all- dusted with powdered sugar.

Cake: Coconut Cake

Preparation: 10 minutes, Cook Time: 55 minutes
Recipe from Pamela Eden.

My Dad gave me this recipe. He and his mom used to make this for afternoon tea.

1 1/2 cups flour
1 (7-ounce) package flaked Baker's Angel Flake Coconut

6 ounces margarine
3/4 cup sugar
3 eggs beaten

Pre-heat oven to 350F. Grease an 8 x4" loaf pan. Cream together sugar and margarine. Add the remaining ingredients and mix until everything is moistened. Bake in a moderate (350F) oven for 55 minutes. Test with toothpick in center of cake comes out clean.

Cake: Gingered Apple Upside-Down Cake

Preparation: 30 minutes, Cook Time: 30 minutes

Source: tasteofhome.com

1/4 cup butter, cubed
1/4 cup packed brown sugar
1 tablespoon finely chopped crystallized ginger
2 large apples, peeled and cut into 1/8-in. slices
BATTER
1/4 cup butter, softened

2/3 cup packed brown sugar
2 eggs
1 teaspoon vanilla extract
1- 1/2 cup all-purpose flour
2 teaspoons baking powder
1 teaspoon ground ginger
1/4 teaspoon salt
1/2 cup 2% milk

Preheat oven to 375°. Place butter in a 9-in. round baking pan; heat in oven until melted. Tilt pan to coat bottom and sides. Sprinkle brown sugar and ginger onto bottom of pan. Arrange apple slices in circles over brown sugar mixture. For batter, in a large bowl, beat butter and brown sugar until blended. Add eggs, one at a time, beating well after each addition. Beat in vanilla. In another bowl, whisk flour, baking powder, ginger and salt; add to creamed mixture alternately with milk. Spoon over apples. Bake 30-35 minutes or until a toothpick inserted in center comes out clean. Cool 10 minutes before inverting onto a serving plate. Serve warm. Yield: 8 servings.

Cake: Golden Fruitcake

Preparation: 30 minutes, Cook Time: 1 hr   Yield: 2 standard loaves

Recipe by Pamela Eden (from King Arthur Flour). For those of us who love fruit cake- this one has proven easy to make and received positive reviews. It's moist and not too sweet.

2 cups raisins golden
1 cup dried cranberries
1 cup dried apricot chopped
1 cup candied lemon peel
1 3/4 cups candied red glaceed cherries
3/4 cup brandy or rum or whiskey
CAKE
1 cup unsalted butter
1 3/4 cups sugar

1/4 cup light corn syrup
2 teaspoons baking powder
1 teaspoon salt
1/2 teaspoon ground nutmeg
1 teaspoon vanilla extract
5 large eggs
3 3/4 cups unbleached all purpose flour
1 cup milk
2 cups diced pecans or walnuts (optional)

To Prepare Fruit: Combine the dried fruit (except for the candied cherries) with liquid in a bowl. Cover and let mixture steep overnight. Pre-heat over to 300F. Lightly grease the loaf pans of your choice: two 8 1/2" x 4 1/2" loaf pans or five 7" baker pans or six 7" paper "bake & give" pans.

To Prepare the cake: In a large bowl, beat together the butter, sugar, corn syrup, baking powder, salt, and flavors. Beat in the eggs one at a time. Stir in the flour alternately with the milk. Add the undrained fruit, the candied cherries and nuts. Spoon the batter into the lightly greased baking pans, filling them 3/4 full. Bake the cakes for 50 - 80 minutes depending on the size of the pans. Smaller pans will bake for a shorter time. When done, the cakes will be a light golden brown all over and a cake tester inserted into the center will come out clean. Remove the cakes from the oven. Brush with brandy or liquor of your choice while warm. When completely cooled, wrap well and let reset at least 24 hours (or for up to 1 month, brushing with liquor or flavored syrup weekly) before serving.

Cake: Noni's Cake

Recipe by Kathleen Jusko

1 box yellow cake mix
1 can large mandarin orange
water
FILLING

1 (6-ounce) package instant vanilla pudding
1 (16-ounce) can crushed pineapple chunks
1 package whipped cream

CAKE: Mix the cake mix, mandarin oranges with juice and sufficient water to make required amount on the box. Make three 8 inch round layers & bake as instructed on cake mix box.

FILLING: Sprinkle instant vanilla powder over large can crushed pineapple in a bowl till well blended and dissolved. Fold whipped cream into this mix. Spread between 3 layers of cake and on top.

Cake: Pudding Cake

Recipe from Kathleen Jusko

1 box cake mix
1 (4-ounce) package non-instant vanilla
   pudding or chocolate pudding (must be
   cooked type of pudding mix)

milk chocolate chips
ground nuts

Grease the bottom of a 9 x 13 pan. Layer the dry cake mix over bottom of pan. Cook pudding according to package directions. Stir into cake mix. Sprinkle with chocolate chips and nuts. Bake 25 minutes at 350F.

Cake: Pumpkin Cheesecake

Recipe by Marie Gelsomino

1 cup crushed ginger snap
3 tablespoons butter
2 tablespoons sugar
FILLING
3 (8-ounce) packages cream cheese softened

1-1/2 cup sugar
4 eggs one at a time
1 cup solid pumpkin canned
1 teaspoon cinnamon
1 teaspoon ginger

Grease an 8-1/2" springform pan. Combine crust ingredients, press into bottom of pan. Combine cream cheese and sugar. Add eggs. one at a time to cream cheese mixture beating well after each addition. Add pumpkin pie spices to cream cheese mixture and mix well. Pour into springform pan. Place pan in a larger pan with hot water 1-1/2" deep. Bake at 325F until done when cheesecake starts to shrink. Approx 1 hour. Chill for 4 hours or overnight in refrigerator.

Cake: Rhubarb Dessert Cake

Makes 12 servings

Cook Time: 30 minutes
Recipe by Kathleen Jusko

2 tablespoons melted butter
1 cup packed brown sugar
4 cups sliced rhubarb fresh or frozen
1 1/2 cups sugar
1 1/2 cups all purpose flour
1 1/2 teaspoons baking powder

1/8 teaspoon salt
3 eggs
1/2 cup water
1 teaspoon vanilla extract
whipped cream or vanilla ice cream

In a greased 13 x 9 inch baking pan combine butter and brown sugar. Top with rhubarb. In large bowl combine sugar, flour, baking powder and salt. In another bowl, whisk the eggs, water and vanilla. Stir into the dry ingredients until just moistened. Pour over rhubarb. Back at 350F for 30- 35 minutes or until cake spring back when lightly touched. Cool for 10 minutes on a wire rack. Serve warm or at room temp with whipped cream or ice cream.

Cake: Ricotta Orange Pound Cake (Giada)

Recipe from Pamela Eden

1 1/2 cups cake flour
2 1/2 teaspoons baking powder
1 teaspoon kosher salt
1 1/2 sticks butter at room temp
1 1/2 cups whole mile ricotta cheese
1 1/2 cups + 1 Tablespoon sugar

3 large eggs
1 teaspoon vanilla extract
1 orange zested
2 tablespoons amaretto
1/2 cup powdered sugar (for dusting top)

Pre-heat oven to 350F. Grease 9 x 5 x 3 loaf pan with butter.

In Medium bowl combine the flour, baking powder & salt. Using a mixer cream the butter, ricotta and sugar till light and fluffy. Add eggs 1 at a time with the mixer running. Add vanilla, orange zest and amaretto til incorporated. Add flour mix a little at a time till incorporated. (don't over beat). Pour into pan and bake 45 - 50 minutes. Cool on rack before removing from pan and dusting top with powdered sugar.

Patti Tivnan

Cake: Sex in a Bowl!

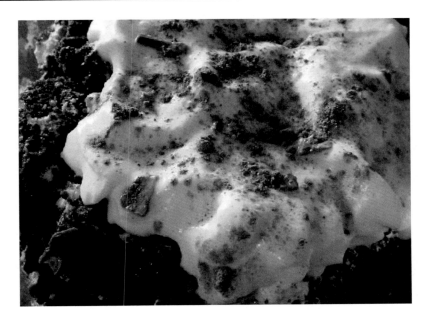

Recipe and photo from Patti Tivnan

Always a Hit! :)

1 box chocolate cake mix
2 packages large chocolate instant pudding
& pie filling mix

1 package cool whip
4 large Heath Candy Bars (or Butterfinger or toffee bits)

Follow the directions on the boxes to make the chocolate pudding and 2 round cakes (8 or 9 inch depending on the size of your trifle dish). Crush the candy bars and set aside. In a glass trifle dish- layer the ingredients by first placing a small amount of pudding on the bottom, followed by a chocolate cake, layer of chocolate pudding, layer of crushed candy bar, layer of cool whip, the second chocolate cake, pudding, candy, and cool whip until the ingredients are finished.

The size of your dessert depends on the size of your dish. Two chocolate cakes usually is enough to complete the dessert. Just remember to finish with cool whip and sprinkle of crushed candy bar on top.

Cake: Tunnel of Fudge Cake

Preparation: 15 minutes, Cook Time: 45 min
Recipe by Pamela Eden

CAKE
1 3/4 cups softened butter (3 1/2 sticks)
1 cup granulated sugar
1/2 cup firmly packed light brown sugar
1 teaspoon vanilla extract
1/2 teaspoon salt
2 ounces unsweetened chocolate melted
6 large eggs

2 cups confectioners' sugar
2 1/4 cups all purpose flour
1/2 cup unsweetened cocoa powder
2 cups chopped pecans
GLAZE
1/2 cup heavy whipping cream
1 tablespoon butter
1/2 cup semi-sweet chocolate chips

Preheat oven to 350F. Grease and flour a 12 cup fluted tube pan or 10 in tube pan. For the cake - place the butter in a large bowl. Beat with an electric mixer set on medium high speed until whipped, about 1 minute. Add the granulated and brown sugars, vanilla and salt. Beat until light and fluffy- about 2 minutes. Add the melted chocolate. Beat in the eggs, 1 at a time until the mixture is smooth. Stir in the confectioners sugar. Combine the flour and cocoa in a medium bowl. Gently stir into the butter mixture. Stir in the pecans. Pour the batter into the prepared pan. Bake until the surface is dry and the edge begins to pull away from the pan, 45 minutes - 1 hour. Transfer to a wire rack to cool completely, 3 -4 hours. Invert the cake onto a serving platter. Remove the pan. For the glaze- place the cream and butter in a small saucepan. Bring to a boil. Remove from heat. Stir in the chocolate chips until smooth. Let cool slightly. Drizzle over cake. Serve.

Cake: $100 Cake

Cook Time: 45 minutes
Recipe from Maureen Heritage

1-1/2 cup sugar
3 cups flour
3/4 cup cocoa powder
3 teaspoons baking powder

3/4 teaspoon salt
1-1/2 cup mayonnaise
1-1/2 cup boiling water
1-1/2 teaspoon vanilla extract

Sift dry ingredients 4 times. Add mayo, water & vanilla. Bake 45 minutes at 350F in two greased 9" round pans or a greased 13 x 9" pan.

Cobbler: Blackberry Cobbler

Recipe from Marie Gelsomino

FILLING
3 cups fresh or frozen blackberries
1 cup sugar
1/4 teaspoon ground cinnamon
3 tablespoons cornstarch
1 cup cold water
1 tablespoon butter

TOPPING
1 1/2 cups flour
1 tablespoon sugar
1 1/2 teaspoons baking powder
1/2 teaspoon salt
1/2 teaspoon cold butter
1/2 cup 2% milk

Pre-heat oven to 350F. Grease an 8" baking dish. In a large sauce pan, combine blackberries, sugar and cinnamon. Cook and stir until boiling. Combine cornstarch and water until smooth. Stir into fruit mixture. Bring to a boil. Cook and stir for 2 minutes or until thickened. Pour into prepared baking dish. Dot with butter pats. For Topping: combine flour, sugar, baking powder and salt. Cut in butter until mixture is coarse & crumbly. Stir in milk to create sticky dough. Drop by tablespoonfuls onto hot berry mix. Bake uncovered for 30 minutes or until browned on top. Serve warm.

Cobbler: Blueberry Buckle

Cook Time: 45 minutes
Recipe from Maureen Heritage

3/4 cup sugar
1/4 cup soft shortening
1 egg
1/2 cup milk
2 cups flour
2 teaspoons baking powder
1/2 teaspoon salt

2 cups blueberries
TOPPING
1/2 cup sugar
1/3 cup flour
1/2 teaspoon cinnamon
1/4 cup soft butter

Mix shortening, sugar & egg. Stir in milk, sift together salt, baking powder and flour. Add to egg mixture. Carefully blend in the blueberries. Spread batter in greased 9" square pan.

Topping: Mix together and sprinkle over cake. Bake at 350F for 45 minutes.

Cobbler: Blueberry Cobbler

Preparation: 15 minutes, Cook Time: 35 minutes
Recipe by Kathleen Jusko

1/2 cup butter
1 cup sugar
1 cup flour
1 1/2 teaspoons baking powder

1/2 teaspoon salt
1 cup milk
2 cups blueberries

Preheat oven to 350F. Slice butter, sprinkle across bottom of baking disk and place in oven to melt. Mix together dry ingredients, then stir in milk. Pour batter into melted butter and scatter fruit over top. Bake uncovered 30 -40 minutes.

Cobbler: Apple or Peach Macaroon

Cook Time: 45 minutes
Recipe from Annie Robertson

3 large (or 6 small) apples
2 tablespoons butter softened
1 cup sugar
2 eggs
1 cup flour

1 tablespoon baking powder
1/2 teaspoon salt
1/2 teaspoon vanilla extract
1/2 teaspoon almond extract

Pre-heat oven to 350F. Peel and core apples and place sliced fruit in 8x8 baking pan. Cream butter, sugar and eggs. Add flour and baking powder. Add salt, vanilla and almond extract to batter. Spread batter over fruit and bake 45 minutes at 350F.

annie Robertson

Cookie Sheet Tart

Recipe by Deette Little

2 cups unbleached all purpose flour
2 tablespoons sugar
2 sticks softened butter or margarine
2 (8-ounce) packages softened cream cheese
2 cups powdered sugar

1 (8-ounce) package frozen whipped topping thawed
1 (16-ounce) can cherry pie filling or blueberry pie filling

Pre-heat oven to 350F. Mix flour and sugar together. Cut in the two sticks of butter or margarine until the mixture is crumbly. Press into a cookie sheet and bake at 350 for about 20 minutes or until golden brown. Let cool. Cream the 2 packages of cream cheese and 2 cups of powdered sugar. Spread on cooled crust. Spread thawed whipped topping on top of the cream cheese. Top with pie filling. Refrigerate until ready to serve.

Patti Tivnan

Cookies: Brownie Roll-Out Cookies

Cook Time: 11 minutes   Yield: 65 cookies

Recipe & Photo from Kathy Rupff (source USA Weekend Magazine)

3 cups all purpose flour plus more for countertop
2/3 cup unsweetened cocoa
3/4 teaspoon salt
1/2 teaspoon baking powder

16 tablespoons (2 sticks) unsalted butter softened
1 1/2 cups sugar
2 large eggs
1 teaspoon vanilla extract

Pre-heat oven to 350F. Whisk flour, cocoa, salt and baking powder in a bowl and set aside. Beat butter and sugar with electric mixer until fluffy. Add eggs one at a time, scraping down the bowl. Mix in vanilla. Gradually mix in the dry ingredients. Wrap dough in plastic and chill for at least 1 hour.

Roll out cookie dough on a floured counter. Cut into desired shapes, brushing extra deposits of flour off the top of the cookies. (the flour does disappear once baked, so don't overly fret if they go into the oven looking a little white).   Bake on a parchment lined baking sheet for 8 -11 minutes (8 for 1/8" thick cookies or 11 for 1/4" cookies) until the edges are firm and the centers are slightly soft and puffed. Transfer to a wire rack to cool.

Yield: 65 cookies, 1 1/2 inches wide from 1/4 thick dough.

Kathy Rupff

Cookies: Chocolate Caramel Bars

Preparation: 15 minutes, Cook Time: 25 minutes
Recipe by Pamela Eden

Yield: 16 bars

- 1 (9-ounce) package Keebler Chocolate Wafers crushed
- 1 (7-ounce) package sweetened flaked coconut
- 1 cup semisweet chocolate chips
- 1 cup white chocolate chips
- 1 cup pecans chopped
- 1 (6-ounce) can sweetened condensed milk
- 24 carmel filled Hershey kisses or Rolo bites halved
- 10 tablespoons unsalted butter melted

Heat oven to 350F. Line a 13 x 9 x 2 baking pan with nonstick foil. Crush 1 package of chocolate wafer cookies and stir together with melted butter. Press evenly into prepared pan. Bake at 350 for 5 minutes. Cool slightly on wire rack. In a large bowl, combine the flaked coconut, chocolate chips, pecans and can of condensed milk. Distribute evenly over the cookie crust. Scatter 24 halved carmel filled candies over top. Bake at 350 for 18 - 20 minutes. Cool completely. Refrigerate overnight. Cut into 16 bars with a large knife using a gentle rocking motion.

Cookies: Classic Shortbread

Cook Time: 35 minutes
Recipe from Pamela Eden
This recipe came with my lovely shortbread stoneware cookie pan from Brown Bag Cookie. These cookies are so light -they are barely there. Plan to make 2 batches- because you eat the 1st batch all by yourself.

- 1/2 cup room temp butter
- 1/3 cup powdered sugar unsifted
- 1/4 teaspoon vanilla extract
- 1 cup flour unsifted

Pre-heat the oven to 325F. Cream the butter until it is light. Cream in the powdered sugar, then vanilla. Now work in the flour. Knead the dough on an unfloured board until nice an smooth. Spray the shortbread pan very lightly with a non-stick vegetable oil spray. Firmly press the dough into the shortbread pan. Prick the entire surface with a fork and bake at 325 for about 30 -35 minutes or until lightly browned.

Let the shortbread cool in it's pan for about 10 minutes before you loosen the edges with a knife and flip the pan over onto a wooden cutting board. Cut the shortbread into serving pieces while it is still warm.

Cookies: Date & Nut Bars

Cook Time: 40 minutes
Recipe from Ruth Grabner

- 1/2 cup flour
- 1/4 teaspoon salt
- 1/4 teaspoon baking powder
- 2 eggs
- 1 cup brown sugar
- 1 (7 1/2-ounce) package pitted dates chopped
- 1 cup nuts
- 1/4 cup butter melted
- 1 teaspoon vanilla extract

Pre-heat oven to 325F. Sift flour, salt and baking powder together. Beat egg till light and fluffy. Gradually add sugar while beating. Add dates and nuts which have been cut into small pieces. Add dry ingredients, melted butter and vanilla. Pour into shallow 8x8" pan and bake for 40 minutes

Cookies: Ginger Shortbread

Recipe from Pamela Eden
Another recipe that came with my stoneware shortbread cookie pan... If you love ginger like I do- then you'll love this cookie.

1/2 cup room temp butter
1/4 cup light brown sugar (packed)
3/4 teaspoon ground ginger

2-3 pieces candied ginger root chopped
1 cup flour
1 tablespoon cornstarch

Cream the butter. Cream in the brown sugar and ground ginger. Now work in the flour and cornstarch. Fold in chopped candied ginger root (these really give texture and punch to the cookie's flavor). Knead the dough on an unfloured board until smooth. Spray the shortbread pan very lightly with a non-stick vegetable oil spray. Firmly press the dough into the shortbread pan. Prick entire surface with a fork and bake at 325F for 30 -35 minutes or until lightly browned.

Let the shortbread cool in its pan for about 10 minutes before loosening the edges with a knife and flipping the pan over onto a wooden cutting board.

Cut the shortbread into pieces while it is still warm.

Cookies: No Bake Chocolate Oatmeal Cookies

Yield: 2 dozen

Recipe from Carol Southerland

1 cup sugar
1/4 cup cocoa powder
1/4 cup milk
1/2 stick margarine

1 1/2 cups quick oats
1 tablespoon peanut butter
1/2 teaspoon vanilla extract

Combine sugar, cocoa, milk and margarine in sauce pan over medium heat. Stir until a full boil. Remove from heat and immediately stir in quick oats, peanut butter and vanilla. Drop by Teaspoon-full onto wax paper, makes about 2 dozen cookies. Refrigerate to make cookies set faster.

Patti Tivnan

Cookies: Shortbread (Sugar)

Cook Time: 13 minutes   Yield: 4 dozen

Recipe from Kathy Rupff (Source: Pillsbury Cookbook)

2 cups powdered sugar
2 cups butter softened
2 egg yolk

4 cups flour
1 cup cornstarch

In a large bowl, combine powdered sugar and butter. Beat until light and fluffy. Add egg yolks, blend well. Add flour and cornstarch, stir until mixture forms a smooth dough. Shape 1/2 recipe dough into a 12" roll, 1-1/2 inches in diameter. Wrap roll in waxed paper. Press sides of roll with palm of ahnd to make 3 even sides forming a triangular shape. Press roll against countertop to smooth and flatten sides. Refrigerate until firm. Heat oven to 350F. Slice dough into 1/4 inch slices. Place on ungreased cookie sheets. Bake at 350 for 8 -13 minutes or until lightly browned and set. Prick tops of cookies with fork; remove from cookie sheets to cool on rack. Makes about 4 dozen cookies.

Cookies: Whole-Grain No-Bake Granola Bars

Preparation: 20 minutes   Yield: 24 bars
Source: food.com

2 cups old fashioned oats
1/4 cup roasted almonds chopped
1/4 cup roasted sunflower seed
1/2 cup shredded coconut
1/2 cup dried fruit chopped

1/2 cup peanut butter
1/2 cup brown rice syrup or honey
1 teaspoon vanilla extract
1 cup mini chocolate chips (optional)

Combine cereal, oats, nuts, seeds, coconut and fruit in a large mixing bowl. Heat the peanut butter, syrup and vanilla in a small sauce pan until warm. Pour the mixture into a 9x13 pan or 8x8 (for thicker bars). Pack the mixture down firmly with moist fingers. Sprinkle chocolate chips over top and press in firmly. Cover with plastic wrap. Cool completely. Cut into 24 bars. Wrap individually and store in the refrigerator.

Cookies: Chocolate-Peanut Butter Crunch Bars

Preparation: 10 minutes, Cook Time: 10 minutes

Source: tasteofhome.com

3 cups miniature pretzels, coarsely chopped
10 tablespoons butter, divided
1 package (10-1/2 ounces) miniature marshmallow
3 cups rice krispies

1/2 cup light corn syrup, divided
3/4 cup peanut butter chips
1 cup (6 ounces) semisweet chocolate chips
1/4 cup dry roasted peanut, chopped

Reserve 1/3 cup chopped pretzels. In a large microwave-safe bowl, microwave 6 tablespoons butter on high for 45-60 seconds or until melted. Stir in marshmallows; cook 1 to 1-1/2 minutes or until marshmallows are melted, stirring every 30 seconds. Stir in Rice Krispies and remaining chopped pretzels. Immediately press into a greased 13x9-in. baking pan. In another microwave-safe bowl, combine 2 tablespoons butter and 1/4 cup corn syrup. Microwave, uncovered, on high for 45-60 seconds or until butter is melted, stirring once. Add peanut butter chips; cook 30-40 seconds or until chips are melted, stirring once. Spread over cereal layer. In a microwave-safe bowl, combine the remaining corn syrup and remaining butter. Cook on high for 45-60 seconds or until butter is melted, stirring once. Add chocolate chips; cook 30-40 seconds longer or until chips are melted, stirring once. Spread over top. Sprinkle with peanuts and reserved pretzels; press down gently. Cover and refrigerate 30 minutes or until set. Cut into bars. Store in airtight containers.

Noodle Kugel

Cook Time: 45 minutes.
Recipe from Rona Shick and passed along by Kathleen Jusko

1 pound broad egg noodle
1 can fruit cocktail
1 cup sour cream
4 ounces cream cheese
1/4 pound butter

1/4 cup sugar
1 teaspoon baking soda
7 eggs
1/2 teaspoon vanilla extract
cinnamon for top

Cook noodles to al dente. Drain. Combine sour cream and baking soda in a bowl and let stand. Cream butter and sugar together. Add cream cheese and sour cream mixture and beat. Add eggs one at a time until thoroughly blended. Add vanilla. Combine mix with cooked noodles and blend in fruit cocktail using most of the juice. Place in buttered lasagna pan and sprinkle with cinnamon. Bake at 350 for 45 minutes or until golden brown on top.

Pie: Applesauce Pie

Preparation: 5 minutes, Cook Time: 45 minutes
Recipe by Pamela Eden | Source: www.pallensmith.com

This pie can be made quickly any time of year. Just mix applesauce with eggs, sugar and cinnamon, pour into a pie shell and bake!

1 9 inch unbaked Pillsbury Pie Crust, Regular
3 eggs
5 tablespoons sugar
1/2 teaspoon cinnamon

1/4 teaspoon vanilla extract
2 cups unsweetened Musselman's Chunky Apple Sauce Home Style
1 tablespoon butter softened

Pre-heat oven to 450F. Place your pie shell in a 9 inch pie pan. I use a pre-made crust if I am in a hurry. Rub the crust with softened butter and place in the refrigerator until the filling is ready. Combine the sugar, cinnamon, and eggs. Beat until smooth. Fold the applesauce and vanilla into the egg mixture and stir until well blended. Remove pie shell from refrigerator and pour in filling. Sprinkle top of pie with remaining 1/4 tsp of cinnamon and place pie in a pre-heated oven at 450F for 15 minutes. Reduce heat to 350F and bake for an additional 30 minutes or until the center of the pie is set.

Note: this can also be made using a graham cracker crust. Sprinkle a little graham cracker on top prior to baking.

Pie: Blueberry Pie

Recipe from Pat Olds

1 Nabisco Honey Made Graham Pie Crust
4 cups fresh blueberries
3/4 cup sugar

1/3 cup flour
1/3 teaspoon cinnamon
1 tablespoon lemon juice

Put 2 cups of Blueberries into a saucepan and cook with sugar, flour, cinnamon and lemon juice. Cook together and stir to keep it from burning until it starts to come to a boil. then pour into the pie crust. Wash the rest of the berries and place the berries on top of the filling. Can be served warm or cold.

Pie: Butter Tarts

Cook Time: 35 minutes
Yield: 12 tarts

Recipe by Pamela Eden. This recipe was handed down from my grandmother. The tarts are easy to make and taste rich and decadent.

1 cup sugar
1/4 cup butter
2 eggs
1 cup Sunmaid Zante Currants or seedless raisens

1 tablespoon vinegar
1/2 teaspoon vanilla extract
1 box refrigerated pie crust

Pre-heat oven to 450F. Cream butter. Add sugar and mix thoroughly. Add eggs, currants and flavoring-beat well. Line cupcake tins with pie crust pastry. Fill each pastry shell 1/2 to 3/4 full with butter mixture. Bake 10 minutes at 450F THEN REDUCE temp to 350F for 20 -25 minutes until filling is firm and pastry crust is nice brown.

Pie: Eggnog Pumpkin Pecan Pie

Preparation: 40 minutes, Cook Time: 50 minutes

Makes 8 servings

Yield: 1 pie

Recipe from Pamela Eden | Source: tasteofhome.com

This pie is the best combination and if you can let it rest overnight before serving so the flavors have time to mature. You can use ready made pie crust if you don't have time to make the crust from scratch, but if you do use pre-made pasty- then be sure to rub the pie pastry with butter to "waterproof" it.

1 1/4 cups all-purpose flour
1/4 teaspoon salt
3 tablespoons shortening cubed
3 tablespoons cold butter cubed
3 to 4 tablespoons cold water
FILLING:
2 eggs
1 can (15 ounces) solid-pack pumpkin
1 cup dairy or canned eggnog
1/2 cup sugar

1 teaspoon ground cinnamon
1/2 teaspoon salt
1/2 teaspoon ground ginger
1/2 teaspoon ground nutmeg
1/4 teaspoon ground cloves
TOPPING:
1/2 cup packed brown sugar
2 tablespoons butter softened
1/2 cup chopped pecans

Pre-heat oven to 350F. Directions In a food processor, combine flour and salt; cover and pulse to blend. Add shortening and butter; cover and pulse until mixture resembles coarse crumbs. While processing, gradually add water until dough forms a ball. Wrap in plastic wrap. Refrigerate for 1 to 1-1/2 hours or until easy to handle. Roll out pastry to fit a 9-in. pie plate. Transfer pastry to pie plate. Trim pastry to 1/2 in. beyond edge of plate; flute edges. In a large bowl, whisk the eggs, pumpkin, eggnog, sugar, cinnamon, salt, ginger, nutmeg and cloves until blended. Pour into crust. In a small bowl, beat brown sugar and butter until crumbly, about 2 minutes. Stir in pecans; sprinkle over filling. Bake at 350° for 50-60 minutes or until a knife inserted near the center comes out clean. Cool on a wire rack. Refrigerate leftovers. Yield: 8 servings.

Kathleen Jusko

Pie: Fresh Raspberry Pie

Recipe from Marie Gelsomino

1 pie crust (top & bottom)
Filling
1-1/3 cup sugar
2 tablespoons quick cooking tapioca
2 tablespoons cornstarch
5 cups fresh or frozen raspberries thawed

1/2 teaspoon lemon juice
1 tablespoon butter
Topping
1 tablespoon milk
1 tablespoon sugar

Prepare pie crust (top and bottom crust) if not using refrigerated pie dough. In a large bowl, combine the sugar, tapioca, cornstarch and raspberries. Let stand for 15 minutes. Add raspberry filling to pie crust. Dot with butter. Fit top crust onto pie. Trim, seal and flute edges. Cut slits in top to vent steam. Brush top crust with milk and sprinkle with sugar. Bake at 350F for 50 -55 minutes or until crust is golden brown and filling is bubbling. Cool on wire rack.

Pie: Spiced Rhubarb Tart

Cook Time: 20 minutes
Recipe from Pamela Eden

rhubarb
sugar
1/4 teaspoon ground ginger
1/4 teaspoon ground cinnamon

1/2 ounce butter
2 tablespoons flour
1/2 ounce sugar
1 pastry crust

Line a deep enamel plate with pastry. Cook rhubarb to a pulp, adding as little water as possible. Sweeten to taste and add ground ginger and cinnamon. Allow to cool and spread on pastry. Combine flour and sugar. Rub in butter to crumblie. Sprinkle over top of rhubarb filling. Bake at 350F for 20 minutes or until top becomes crisp.

Pie: Super Quick Pie - Gluten Free

Recipe from Merle Morse

1 box Chex Cereal
1 can pie filling (your favorite fruit)

1/2 cup walnuts, pecans or almonds chopped

Cover bottom of pie plate with Chex Cereal. Spread pie filling over cereal base. Sprinkle nuts on top. Refrigerate for 4 hours or overnight.

Pie: Tawny Pumpkin Pie

Cook Time: 50 minutes
Yield: 6 -8 servings

Recipe from Jody Cooke
"I have been making this recipe for Thanksgiving for over 20 yrs. It's my husband and daughter's favorite. Even if we travel somewhere I bring this pie. The secret is in the fresh pumpkin-- even non pumpkin pie lovers will convert. We serve it chilled with lots and lots of fresh whipped cream and a dash of cinnamon on top.

1-1/4 cup fresh pumpkin cooked
3/4 cup sugar
1/2 teaspoon salt
1/4 teaspoon ground ginger
1 teaspoon ground cinnamon
1 teaspoon all-purpose flour

2 eggs slightly beaten
1 cup evaporated milk
2 tablespoons water
1 teaspoon vanilla extract
1 pinch nutmeg optional
1 9 inch pie crust unbaked

Combine pumpkin, flour, sugar, salt and spices in mixing bowl. Add eggs. Mix well. Add evaporated milk, water and vanilla and mix. Pour into pastry lined pan. bake in pre-heated hot oven (475F) for 15 minutes. Reduce heat to moderate (350F) and bake for 35 minutes longer or until set. Makes 6 -8 servings.

Pie: Yogurt Flan

Cook Time: 12 minutes

Recipe and photographic proof by Pamela Eden

1/2 can sweetened condensed milk
500 grams plain yogurt
1/4 cup lemon juice
1 teaspoon vanilla extract
1/2 cup butter or margarine

1/4 cup light brown sugar
1 cup flour
1/4 cup quick cooking grits
1/4 cup chopped walnuts
mixed fruit fresh or canned

Pre-heat oven to 375F. Combine sweetened condensed milk, yogurt, lemon juice and vanilla in a small bowl. Chill to thicken. Cream together the butter and brown sugar. Add flour, quick oats and walnuts and mix into a dry crumbly mixture. Press dough into a greased pizza pan or cookie sheet. Prick with a fork and bake for 10 -12 minutes. Cool.   Spoon in yogurt filling. Refrigerate overnight before decorating with fruit.

Raspberry Fool

Makes 4 servings

Frozen blueberries or strawberries may be substituted for raspberries with equally delicious results.

1 (10-ounce) package frozen unsweetened raspberries thawed
1/3 cup confectioners' sugar

1/4 cup heavy cream well chilled
1 cup vanilla nonfat Greek yogurt
4 lady fingers

Process half the raspberries in a food processor until smooth. Transfer puree to a fine mesh strainer and strain into a large bowl, pressing liquid out with a rubber spatula. Discard seeds. whisk in confectioners sugar. Stir in remaining raspberries. In a chilled medium sized bowl, whip cream with an electric mixer until soft peaks form. Gently fold in yogurt, then fold in raspberry mixture. Spoon into cocktail glasses and cover with plastic wrap. Chill for at least 1 hour and up to 1 day. Serve garnished with lady finger cookies.

Rice Pudding

Recipe from Pamela Eden

This is a great recipe to use up left over rice. During summer vacations throughout college, I used to work on different farms- and this recipe came from Mrs Rempel, a wonderful woman on a farm in Alberta, Canada.

2 cups milk
2 eggs
1/2 teaspoon vanilla extract
3/4 cup sugar

3/4 cup raisins
2 cups cooked rice
1 teaspoon nutmeg
1/2 teaspoon rum extract (optional)

Pre-heat oven to 375F. Butter sides and bottom of a casserole dish. Beat eggs, add milk, vanilla, nutmeg, sugar and raisins. Mix in cooked rice. Bake for about 30 minutes.

Chapter 9: Beverages

Pamela Eden

Apple Tea

Recipe from Marie Gelsomino

1-2 fragrant apple Winesap or Cortland
6-8 tea bags

1 cup boiling water

Put apples and teabags in an airtight container for several days. Steep teabags in boiling water to desired strength. Serve hot

Banana Smoothie

1 cup orange or pineapple juice
1 banana sliced

1/2 cup plain yogurt
3 froze strawberries or ice cubes

Combine everything in a blender or food processor. Blend until smooth. Makes 1 serving.

Breakfast in a Glass

1 (8-ounce) container lemon or other flavor
   yogurt
1 tablespoon frozen orange juice
   concentrate thawed, undiluted

1 small banana
1 tablespoon wheat germ

Combine everything in a blender. Blend on high 15 -20 seconds or until smooth. Pour into a tall glass. Serve at once.

Hot Apple Punch

Yield: 2 Quarts

Recipe from Marie Gelsomino
(Tasteofhome.com)

1 3" cinnamon stick
10 whole cloves

6 whole allspice
1/2 gallon apple juice

Cook cinnamon sticks, cloves and allspice in a dutch oven with apple juice. Reduce heat and simmer for 30 minutes. Discard spices. Serve hot punch in mugs

Mint Cucumber Cooler

Makes 4 servings

Yield: 1 Quart

Recipe from Pamela Eden

1 pound cucumber (~2 cukes)
1/2 cup fresh lime juice (5-10 limes)
1-1/4 cup packed spearmint leaves

1/4 cup agave or 1/2 c sugar
1-1/4 cup water
ice

Put ingredients except ice into blender. Add enough water to fill blender 3/4 full. Hold lid on blender and puree until smooth. Place fine mesh sieve over bowl and pour puree through it. Press sieve with back of spoon to remove as much liquid as possible. Fill a large pitcher 1/2 with ice cubes. Add the juice and serve with sprigs fo mint and slice of lime.

Orange Cream Soda

Yield: 4 servings

Recipe from Marie Gelsomino
(Tasteofhome.com)

8 scoops vanilla ice cream　　　　　**1/4 teaspoon orange extract**
4 cups orange soda chilled

Chill tall glasses in the freezer. Place 2 scoops ice cream in each of 4 chilled 16 oz glasses. In a large pitcher, combine the soda and extract. Pour over ice cream

Purple People Eater Punch

Recipe from Marie Gelsomino

2 quarts purple grape juice chilled　　　　**2 quarts vanilla ice cream softened**
2 liters club soda chilled

Pour grape juice into a 6 quart punch bowl. Slowly pour in club soda. Gently spoon ice cream into punch bowl and whisk to swirl.

This recipe can be halved for smaller groups. Punch can be transported in a large airtight container with the ice cream on top, unmixed. Pour into punch bowl.

Spiced Hot Apple Cider

Cook Time: 30-60 minutes　　　　　　　　　　　　　　　　　　　　Yield: 1 gallon
Recipe from Pamela Eden

I make this every year at Christmas time and not only does it taste great, it makes the house smell wonderful!

1 gallon apple cider　　　　　　　　**2-3 star anise seeds**
3-4 3" cinnamon sticks　　　　　　　**4-5 slices candied ginger**
1 tablespoon whole cloves

Combine all ingredients in a dutch oven. Boil for 5 minutes (watch it doesn't boil over). Reduce heat to simmer for 30 minutes - 1 hour. (all the spices will fall to the bottom)
Serve hot in mugs.

Vanilla Scented Tea

Yield: 4 servings

Recipe from Marie Gelsomino

(tasteofhome.com)

4 cups water　　　　　　　　**4 teaspoons 3-4 teabags or black tea leaves**
1 vanilla bean

Place water in a large saucepan. Split vanilla bean, scrape seeds into water. Add bean. Bring water just to a boil. Add tea leaves or teabags in a teapot. Pour vanilla water over tea. Cover and steep for 3 minutes or to desired strength. Strain tea, discarding tea leaves and vanilla bean. Tea may be sweetened with sugar or honey.

Chapter 10: Odds N Ends

Dog Biscuits: Honey-Cinnamon Treats

Cook Time: 15 minutes

Painting by Pat Olds

1/2 cup oil
1/2 cup honey
1 teaspoon vanilla extract
1 egg

2 tablespoons milk
2 1/2 cups wheat flour
1 teaspoon baking powder
1/2 teaspoon cinnamon

Pre-heat oven to 375F and Grease a baking sheet. In a large bowl, mix oil, honey, vanilla, cinnamon, milk and egg. Stir in flour and baking powder. Knead on lightly floured surface. Roll out dough to 1/4 -1/2" thick and cut with cookie cutter. Bake 13 - 15 minutes.

Dog Biscuits: Milk Bone Treats

Cook Time: 50 minutes   Yield: 1-1/4 lb of dog biscuits

Recipe from Pamela Eden courtesy of Blairstown Dog Park. Drawing of Tippy by Pat Olds.

3/4 cup hot water   **1/3 cup butter**
1/2 cup dry milk powder   **1 teaspoon salt**
1 egg beaten   **3 cups whole wheat flour**

Preheat oven to 325F. In a large bowl pour the hot water over the butter. Stir in powdered milk, salt and egg. Add flour 1/2 cup at a time. Knead for a few minutes to form a stiff dough. Roll to 1/2 inch thickness. Cut into bone shapes. Bake for 50 minutes. Cool. They will be quite hard. Makes about 1-1/4lbs of biscuits.

Dog Biscuits: Oatmeal Pumpkin Treats

Cook Time: 60 minutes

Painting of Charlie by Pat Olds

1 1/2 cups wheat flour	**2 teaspoons cinnamon**
2 tablespoons dry milk	**3 tablespoons vegetable oil**
1 1/2 cups white flour	**1/2 cup canned pumpkin**
1/2 cup rolled oats	**1/2 cup water**
1 teaspoon baking powder	**1 tablespoon water**

Heat oven to 250F. Mix everything in a mixer. Roll out into rectangular sheet 1/4" thick. Use a cookie cutter or pizza cutter. Bake at 250F for 60 minutes. Turn off oven and leave cookies in oven overnight so they become hard and crispy.

Dog Biscuits: Whole Wheat & Bacon Treats

Cook Time: 50 minutes   Yield: 1-1/4 lbs dog biscuits

recipe from Pamela Eden courtesy of Blairstown Dog Park. Painting of Silver by Pat Olds.

3/4 cup hot beef broth
1/2 cup dry milk powder
1 tablespoon minced garlic
1/4 cup cooked chopped bacon
3 cups whole wheat flour

1/3 cup butter
1/2 teaspoon salt
1 tablespoon parsley flakes
1 egg beaten

Preheat oven to 325F. In a large bowl, combine broth and butter. Add powdered milk, salt, garlic, parsley and egg. Stir in flour in 1/2 cup increments, mixing well after each addition. Knead dough for 3-4 minutes and roll out to 1/2 inch thickness. Cut into desired shapes. Place on greased cookie sheet and bake 50 minutes. Remove from oven and let dog biscuits cool until dry and hard. It's ok to leave them in the oven after turning it off. Makes approx 1-1/4 dry dog biscuits.

English Muffin Bread

Preparation: 45 minutes, Cook Time: 25 minutes   Yield: 2 loaves
Recipe from Kathleen Jusko

5 1/2 - 6 cups flour measured by spooning
   flour lightly into cup.
2 packages Active dry yeast
1 tablespoon sugar
2 teaspoons salt

1/4 teaspoon baking soda
2 cups milk
1/2 cup water
cornmeal

Combine 3 Cup flour, yeast, sugar, salt and soda. heat liquids until very warm (120F). Add to dry mixture. Beat well. Stir in enough additional flour to make a stiff batter. Spoon into two 8-1/2 x 4-1/2" pans that have been greased and sprinkled with cornmeal. Sprinkle tops of loaves with cornmeal. Cover loaves and let rise in warm place for 45 minutes. Bake at 400F for 25 minutes. Remove from pans immediately onto wire rack to cool.

Festive Stuffing
Recipe by Pamela Eden

I always make this stuffing to go along with the turkey at Thanksgiving or Christmas. Since it's made outside the turkey, it can be made in advance and reheated when ready to serve.

1 box corn bread stuffing
orange juice
1 (3.4-ounce) package shelled roasted
**   chestnuts chopped**
1 - 2 tablespoon apricot or orange
**   marmalade**

5-6 dried apricots halves chopped
1/4 cup golden raisins
5-6 pitted dates chopped
1 tablespoon finely chopped candied ginger
**   (optional)**
maple syrup (optional)

Make Corn bread stuffing according to package instructions, but substitute orange juice for water. Add 6-8 chopped chestnuts, chopped dried apricots, golden raisins, dates, 1 to 2 large spoons of apricot or orange marmalade and candied ginger (optional). Mix well. Cover and hold over low heat for 10 minutes to allow flavors to mingle before serving.

Sometimes I also add a swirl of maple syrup on top of the stuffing before dishing out.

Store the remaining chestnuts in the package in the refrigerator and use them (chopped) in salads, chili or soup. I like these ready to eat chestnuts because while their flavor is very mild - they add a nice filling density.

HELPFUL HINTS

Hint 1- Spray measuring cup/ spoon with non-stick cooking spray BEFORE measuring honey, molasses or agave and you won't have any trouble putting everything measured into the recipe.

Hint 2 - Removing white heat or liquid marks from wood table tops:
Mix a small dollop of paste-style toothpaste with an equal measure of baking soda until smooth.
With a damp papertowel, rub the toothpaste mixture over the white mark until thoroughly coated.
Using a clean portion of the damp paper towel,wipe away the toothpaste mixture.
Apply a furniture wax to protect wood finish.

Hint 3 - Removing stains from fabrics:
Use Alcohol to remove grass, grease and soft drink stains.
Use Borax to remove juice stains.
Use hydrogen peroxide to remove scorch marks and chocolate.
Use Lemon juice to remove ink, iodine and rust.
Use white vinegar to remove alcohol, deodorants, coffee and glue.

Photos by Patti Tivnan

Patti Tivnan

Home Made Antibacterial Foaming Hand Soap

Yield: 1 Gallon

Recipe from Pamela Eden

Antibacterial, Non-drying, Easy to make, Cost saving - What's not to Love?

1 gallon water, divided
1 bar castile soap grated
2 tablespoons vegetable glycerin

2 tablespoons olive oil (or grapeseed, almond or jojoba)
20 drops Tea Tree or lemon essential oil (or Nutribotic GSE)

Bring 4 cups of water to a boil (in a saucepan or dutch oven no longer used for food). Add grated bar of castile soap. Stir continually until dissolved.
Cool for 15 minutes and add vegetable glycerin and olive oil. When completely cool add essential oils and pour back into gallon container, cap and invert to mix.

Dispense into FOAMING Soap Dispensers.

Home made Moisterizing Hand Balm

Yield: six 4.25 oz jars

6 ounces soy wax
8 ounces coconut oil
6 ounces cocoa butter unscented

4 ounces sweet almond oil
lavender essential oil

Melt soy wax on double boiler (or microwave in 15 -20 sec bursts). Once melted, add coconut oil and cocoa butter. Continue to heat and stir mixture until everything is liquid, then add sweet almond oil. Add 20 drops (~1mL) lavender essential oil to give balm a nice fragrance. Pour solution into small containers with snug fitting lids.

Home-made Lip Balm

16 ozs will make about 100 lip balm tubes.

16 ounces natural melt & pour lip balm base available from rusticescentuals.com
Melt lip balm base in a double boiler or microwave (in a pyrex dish with no covering). Melt for 15-30 second increments stirring thoroughly. When melted completely - use lip balm flavor oils at <3% usage rate(*). Use pipettes to transfer to lip balm tubes wait til lip balm has cooled a bit before transferring (no hotter than 115C). Cap tubes once cooled completely. Note if only making a small batch, a rubber band around a group of tubes works great to hold everything together upright while you fill them.

(*) multipy product weight by 0.03. The result is the weight of flavor oil to use. This is the max amount to use.

"Flavor" or "Fragrance" is all thats needed on label for ingredients.

Kathleen Jusko

How to Freeze Cheesecake

Guidance from Marie Gelsomino

Cheesecakes can be frozen for 4-6 months.
Freeze cheesecakes without the toppings.

Wrap cooled cheesecake in plastic wrap. Wrap tightly in aluminum foil. Place cheesecake in a 1 gallon freezer bag or larger. Thaw cheesecake in refrigerator at least 24 hours before serving. Add toppings after cheesecake has thawed completely.

How to Freeze Pies

Fruit pies can be frozen either before or after they're baked. Keep in mind, pies with custard, cream or meringue toppings don't freeze well. Most fruit pies are double crusted. If you'd like to freeze them, you'll need to follow a few extra steps to preserve them.

First brush the inside of the unbaked bottom pastry with an egg white to keep it from getting soggy. Add 1-1/2 times more cornstarch, flour or tapioca than the recipe calls for. For fruit fillings that brown easily (such as apples), toss the fruit with a n acid such as lemon juice. Brush the top pastry with an egg wash, but don't cut venting slits at this point. Tightly wrap and freeze. Unbaked fruit pies can be frozen for up to 4 months.

Bake frozen pies unthawed. First unwrap the pie, cut slits in the top pastry and bake at 425F for 15 minutes, then reduce the heat and bake at 375 for 30-45 minutes or until bubbly.

To freeze a baked pie: Cool the pie completely, then wrap and seal in freezer plastic wrap. To serve, unwrap the pie and refrigerate until thawed, then let the pie stand at room temperature for 30 minutes. Bake at 350F for 30-40 minutes or until warm. Freeze baked pies for up to 4 months.

How to Make Truffles

The following recipe is for Mocha Truffles. Let your imagination go and roll the truffles in finely ground pistachios or coconut etc.

2/3 cup heavy cream	**2/3 cup confectioners' sugar**
2 tablespoons coffee liqueur	**1/4 teaspoon salt**
6 ounces semi-sweet baking chocolate	**1/2 cup unsweetened cocoa powder**
8 ounces bittersweet chocolate	**1/2 cup confectioners' sugar**

Line an 8" square pan with nonstick foil. Line a large baking sheet with wax paper. Heat heavy cream and coffee liqueur just to a simmer.

Into a food processor Add semisweet and bittersweet chocolate, 2/3 cup confectioners sugar and salt. Whirl 1 -2 minutes until finely ground. With machine running, add cream mixture in a steady stream. Process until smooth. Scrape into foil lined pan and chill for 1- 1/2 hours. Lift from pan using the foil. cut into 36 pieces. Shape into balls by rolling between hands. Place on wax paper lined sheet. Chill 15 minutes. Re-roll truffles to smooth any rough edges if needed. Sift 1/2 cup unsweetened cocoa powder into one bowl. Place 1/2 cup confectioners sugar into another bowl. Add truffles, a few at a time, toss to coat. Transfer each to a small paper or foil cup. Store in an airtight container up to 1 month.

Jam: Gingered Peach Jam

Cook Time: 30 minutes   Yield: 4 cups
Recipe from Pamela Eden. Source: Familycircle.com

6 large ripe peaches
3 cups sugar
2 tablespoons ginger chopped

1 tablespoon lemon juice
1/2 teaspoon salt

Place peaches in large pot of boiling water for 1 minute. Rinse in cold water and peel. Remove pits and cut into wedges (about 6 cups). Transfer to food processor and pulse until coarsely chopped. In a medium stainless steel saucepan, combine peaches and remaining ingredients. Simmer over medium heat, stirring occasionally until thickened about 30 minutes. Ladle into Mason jars and cool. Refrigerate overnight before using. Store in refrigerator for up to 1 month.

Jam: Orange Blueberry Freezer Jam
Makes 32 servings

Preparation: 25 minutes   Yield: 4 cups

2-1/2 cups sugar
1 medium orange

1-1/2 cup fresh blueberries crushed
1 (3-ounce) pouch liquid fruit pectin

Rinse four clean 1 cup plastic containers with lids with boiling water. Dry thoroughly. Preheat oven to 250F. Place sugar in a shallow baking dish. Bake 15 minutes. Meanwhile, finely grate 1 Tablespoon peel from orange. Peel and chop orange. In a large bowl, crush blueberries one layer at time (a potato masher works well). To the crushed blueberries add the warm sugar, grated peel and chopped orange. Let stand 10 minutes, stirring occasionally. Add pectin, stir constantly for 3 minutes to evenly distribute pectin. Immediately fill all containers to within 1/2 inch of container top. Wipe off top edges of containers, immediately cover with lids. Let stand at room temperature until set, but not longer than 24 hours.   Jam is now ready to use. Refrigerate up to 3 weeks or freeze up to 12 months. Thaw frozen jam in refrigerator before serving.

JeanParry
6-8-01

Perfect Pickled Onion Recipe

Preparation: 25 hours

Pickled onions are eaten with fish and chips, on a Ploughman's Lunch, and savory dishes. Tiny pickling or buttons onions are available in the autumn (Sept) and if prepared and stored are perfect by November/December to eat with cold meats, sandwiches, or cheese & crackers.

2-1/4 pounds pickling onions, peeled (see note below)
4 teaspoons pickling spices or
1/2 teaspoon coriander seeds, 1/2 tsp mustard seed, 1/2 tsp black peppercorns, 1/2 tsp dried chili flakes

1 ounce salt
35 ounces malt vinegar
6 ounces sugar

NOTE: Peeling pickling onions is fiddley and time consuming. To speed up the process top and tail the onions, then place the onions in a large heatproof bowl and pour over boiling water to cover. Leave to cool, and once the water is cool, hey presto, the skins will just rub away. Drain and pat the onions dry. Do not leave in the water once cool or the onions will start to go mushy. Sprinkle the salt over the dry, peeled onions, stir to make sure the salt is distributed and leave overnight. Next day (do not leave longer than overnight if you want your onions to be crisp) rinse the onions and dry with kitchen towel. Place the spices, vinegar and sugar into a large stainless steel pan. Heat to dissolve the sugar but do not boil. Pack the onions into clean, sterilized jars. Pour over the vinegar and spice liquid to fill the jars, make sure each jar has pickling spices in and check there are no air pockets. Seal the jars and leave to cool.

The onions will be ready to eat after about one month or better if kept for two. Once opened store in a refrigerator.

Source: britishfood.about.com

Pickes: Cranberry-Pear Chutney

Recipe from Kathleen Jusko, Painting of Pears by Susan Reynolds.

1 pound fresh or frozen cranberries (4 cups)
2 small pears peeled & chopped (~1-1/2 cup)
1 large onion chopped (~1 cup)
1 cup granulated sugar
1/2 cup packed brown sugar
1/2 cup golden raisins

1 cup water
2 teaspoons ground cinnamon
1 1/2 teaspoons ground ginger
1/4 teaspoon ground cloves
1/4 teaspoon ground allspice

In a 3 quart saucepan, mix all ingredients. Heat to boiling over high heat stirring frequently. Reduce heat to medium and cook for about 20 -25 minutes stirring occasionally until thickened. Cool at room temp at least 2 hours. Chutney will thicken more as it cools. Store in refrigerator up to 2 weeks.

Pickle - India Relish

Preparation: overnight
Recipe from Pamela Eden

Yield: 4-1/2 pints

2 pounds medium cucumbers
2 pounds green tomatoes
2 sweet green peppers chopped
2 sweet red peppers chopped
2 onions finely chopped
1/4 cup white mustard seed
2 cups vinegar
1-1/2 cup sugar

2 teaspoons celery seed
1/4 teaspoon turmeric
1/8 teaspoon ground mace
1/8 teaspoon ground cloves
2 tablespoons hot red hot chili peppers
finely chopped
1 pint cabbage or celery finely cut

Choose firm, green cucumbers about 6 inches long and 1-1/4 inches in diameter and tomatoes that have the whitish color acquired just before ripening. Wash vegetables, remove stems, cores and blemishes. Put quartered tomatoes and cucumbers through a food processor. Put into a glass or enamel bowl, add salt and let stand overnight.

Place in a colander and press out and discard liquid, add next four vegetables measured lightly, then remaining ingredients. Simmer 10 minutes, stirring occasionally. Pour into hot sterilized jars and seal with glass or enamel lined lids.

Pickle: Cranberry & Kumquat Relish

Makes 8 servings

Preparation: 15 - 20 minutes
Recipe from Pamela Eden -

This relish goes perfectly with Ham or Turkey and makes a great change of pace from the usual cranberry sauce.

1 (12-ounce) bag fresh cranberries
1 cup kumquats chopped or thinly sliced
1 cup honey

2 tablespoons crystalized ginger
2 4 inchs cinnamon sticks
1 tablespoon lemon juice

In a 4 Qt sauce pan heat honey, cinnamon sticks and ginger to boiling. Add kumquats and simmer until just soft. With a slotted spoon remove the kumquats and cinnamon sticks, discard the cinnamon sticks. Add cranberries to the honey mixture in the sauce pan and cook until the cranberries burst. Remove from heat, stir in lemon juice and allow to cool. Stir kumquats back into the mixture and spoon into jars. Refrigerate.

Pickles - SAVE THE BRINE!

Pickles on grocery shelves have been cooked in the jars and last about 2 yrs unopened. Refrigerated pickles are not cooked and last 3 months to a year - they have a crisp fresh crunch. After you've eaten all the pickles in the jar - don't toss the juice! Recycle it to make your own pickled vegetables. Add sliced produce to the jar with enough leftover brine to cover the veggies; replace the cap and refrigerate. Soft vegetables (peppers, onions, asparagus, cabbage) will be ready to eat in 2 days. Harder types (cauliflower, carrots, radishes) in 5 days. Pickled veggies will keep in the refrigerator for up to a month.

Pie Crust Mix

Make up your own pie crust mix - store in a covered container and refrigerate. It will keep indefinitely.

6 cups flour   **2-1/2 cups shortening**
1 tablespoon salt

Mix flour and salt. Cut in shortening until crumbly. Store in covered container in the refrigerator.

To make a 9" crust, combine 1-1/2 cups of the mix with 2 -4 TB water.

For a 10" crust, combine 1-3/4 cups mix and 3-5 TB water.

Pie: Assorted Crumb and Nut Crust Recipes

Yield: One 9" crust

Various depending on the particular crust

1) Vanilla Cookie crust: 1-1/2 C cookie crumbs + 1/4 C sugar + 6 TB butter. Bake at 350F for 8 minutes.

2) Gingersnap crust: 1-1/2 C cookie crumbs + 1/4 C sugar + 6 TB butter. Bake at 375F for 6 minutes.

3) Chocolate Nut crust: 3/4 C chocolate wafers + 3/4 C ground nuts (Almond, peanuts, pecan, walnuts or hazelnuts) + 2 TB sugar + 6 TB butter. Chill until firm

4) Coconut crust: 2 C flaked or shredded coconut + 4 TB butter and bake at 325F for 15 -20 minutes.

5) Nut crust: 2C ground nuts (Almond, peanuts, pecan, walnuts or hazelnuts) + 1/4 C sugar in a processor to form a paste. Bake at 375F for 8 minutes.

6) Almond Cookie and Nut crust : 1/2 C crushed amaretti cookies + 1/2 C ground toasted almonds + 1/4 C sugar + 6 TB butter. Bake at 375F for 5 minutes.

7) Graham and Nut crust: 1 C graham crumbs + 1/2 C ground nuts + 1/4 C sugar + 6 TB butter. Bake at 350F for 8 minutes.

Refrigerator Yeast Dough

Preparation: 6 hours
Recipe from Kathleen Jusko

2 packages active dry yeast   **1/2 stick butter or margarine**
2 cups water warm   **1 teaspoon salt**
1/2 cup sugar   **5 1/2 - 6 cups flour**
1 egg slightly beaten

In a large bowl put 2 pkgs of yeast in 1 cup warm water. In smaller bowl put second cup of water (quite a bit warmer) and add the 1/2 cut sugar, 1/2 stick butter and 1 tsp salt. Stir to dissolve sugar, butter and salt. Put a cup of flour into the yeast bowl, add the egg and other cup of water mixture. Work in the flour until a fairly firm dough. Cover with plastic wrap and refrigerate for at least 6 hours or till raised to the top of the bowl. When ready to use, punch down and turn out onto a floured cloth.

This dough can be partly used and remainder put back in refrigerator. Will keep for 7 days.

Gordon Perry

Patti Tivnan

Index

WARREN COUNTY ARTS MEMBERHIP

APPLICATION

PLEASE PRINT CLEARLY

TYPE OF MEMBERSHIP

☐ SINGLE ($25)
☐ FAMILY ($45)

TYPE OF ART OR MEDIA

☐ WATERCOLOR
☐ OILS
☐ ACRYLICS
☐ PHOTOGRAPHY
☐ SCULPTURE
☐ OTHER:

ARTIST SKILL LEVEL

☐ PROFESSIONAL
☐ NON-PROFESSIONAL
☐ APPRECIATES

Are you interested in working on a committee?

☐ Hanging for shows
☐ Hospitality
☐ Publicity
☐ Venue research

Comments:

Name

Address

Phone

Email

Website

Warren County ARTS Membership Application submission

WCARTS
PO Box 420
Washington, NJ 07882

Warren County ARTS Membership Application Form Requirements

Single Membership.........$25 per year

Family Membership.........$45 per year

Dues are collected in March each year, by mail or at the monthly meeting.

Non-Members

A recommended donation of $4.00 is requested for non-members attending monthly meetings/programs.

Membership Application

If you would like to become a member please fill out the application form, make your check to Warren County ARTS, and send application & check to:

WCARTS membership
C/o Pamela Eden
466 State Route 94
Columbia, NJ 07832

Or submit payment along with the application to the treasurer at the next scheduled Warren County ARTS meeting. . For more information regarding membership, contact Pamela Eden at 908-496-4315 or pjeden@yahoo.com

Warren County ARTS Membership Application submission

WCARTS
PO Box 420
Washington, NJ 07882

Warren County ARTS Activities

Some of our activities include the Spring open Art Show, field trips, an annual picnic, off-site member art shows, "paint outs" and photography "shoot-outs".

Other Warren County ARTs extras include a monthly newsletter, a website (http://www.WCARTS.org) and networking with other organizations, such as The Pahaquarry, the Hillcrest camera Club, and the Warren County Cultural and Heritage Commission. The Warren County Cultural and heritage Commission periodically assists with grant funding for our organization's art programs.

Warren County ARTS in Oxford, NJ

Warren County ARTS has an ongoing partnership with the Township of Oxford, NJ to reach out to the public through the arts. Warren County ARTS coordinates a variety of art shows and programs in the Oxford Municipal Art Gallery.

Monthly Meetings

Warren County ARTS meets monthly, at 7pm, on the second Thursday of each month, with the exception of August (when there is no meeting). We get together at the Oxford Township Municipal Art Gallery unless notified otherwise. Each meeting includes a program, which offers to entertain and inform.

Our meetings are open to the public and we welcome everyone and anyone wishing to support the arts. Warren County ARTS recommends a nominal donation of $4.00 for non-members attending our programs.

Warren County ARTS Membership

Supporting the arts in Warren County and the surrounding region

WC ARTS
PO Box 420
Washington, NJ 07882

http://www.WCARTS.org

Made in the USA
Lexington, KY
08 November 2017